MACAULAY

from a painting by JOHN PARTRIDGE *in the National Portrait Gallery*

MACAULAY

by
KENNETH YOUNG

Edited by Ian Scott-Kilvert

PUBLISHED FOR
THE BRITISH COUNCIL
BY LONGMAN GROUP LIMITED

LONGMAN GROUP LTD
Longman House, Burnt Mill, Harlow, Essex

*Associated companies, branches and
representatives throughout the world*

First published 1976
ⓒ Kenneth Young 1976

*Printed in England by
Bradleys, Reading and London*

ISBN 0 582 01263 5

CONTENTS

¶ THOMAS BABINGTON MACAULAY was born on 25 October 1800 at Rothley Temple near Leicester. He died on 28 December 1859 at Kensington and was buried in Westminster Abbey.

MACAULAY

I. INTRODUCTION

FOR THOMAS BABINGTON MACAULAY who made history as
popular as novels, transmuted journalism into literature,
and packed the House of Commons every time he got
up to speak, 'it was roses, roses, all the way' and the larger
stones cast at him were cast only after he was dead. He was
born in 1800. Fame came to him at twenty-five and presented
him, parvenu though he dubbed himself, with a barony two
years before his death in 1859.

His father Zachary Macaulay, who came of a line of
Scottish Ministers of the Kirk, was, wrote James Stephen,
'possessed by one idea and animated by one master passion':
the abolition of slavery. He had been book-keeper and then
manager of an estate in Jamaica, and in the 1790s governed a
charter company then forming a colony in Sierra Leone of
liberated slaves who had fought on the British side in the
American War of Independence. The experience left Zachary
with no illusions; the freed men were slothful and quarrel-
some, egged on by the Black fanatics who called themselves
Methodists. Thomas never forgot his father's tales of Africa;
'I am made sick', he said the year before he died, 'by the cant
and the silly mock reasons of the Abolitionists'. He hated
slavery from the 'bottom of my soul', yet 'the nigger driver
and the negrophile are two odious things to me'.

Thomas Macaulay's mother was the pretty Selina Mills,
daughter of a Quaker bookseller in Bristol, and an admirable
counterpoise to the dour Zachary, 'at once so earnest and so
monotonous'. As her family grew to nine, she made sure that,
amidst the sermon-reading and earnest talk, Thomas and her
other children could romp, play hide-and-seek, and blind-
man's buff, blow horns up and down the stairs, make up
ballads, cap verses and perform charades.

Zachary seldom interfered with the family fun, though he
did nag Thomas to curb his ever-wagging tongue, cease
displaying his opinions so violently, be neat and tidy; and he
banned the reading of poetry and novels in the day-time:

'drinking drams in the morning', he called it. Thomas and his father got on well enough together. Nevertheless, Thomas, according to his sister, 'could not recall an instance in which his father had ever praised him or shown any sense of his abilities'. It was to his mother that Thomas was most deeply attached, and to whom he owed his equability, his good humour and his tenderness.

His childhood was spent among a group of well-to-do, middle-class, Church of England activists known as the Evangelicals, who lived in large houses with plenty of servants around Clapham Common, a south London suburb. The austere, heavy-browed Zachary was their magus. William Wilberforce, Henry Thornton, M.P., Lord Teignmouth, Governor-General of India, and the irascibly brilliant Lord Brougham were their chiefs. Later came the Grants, Stephens, Venns, from whom sprang a pervasive intellectual aristocracy. Dr Johnson long ago on his Scottish tour had met Thomas's great uncle Kenneth and had spotted the type: 'He set out with a prejudice against prejudice, and wanted to be a smart thinker'.

The Clapham Sect, as they came to be known, were, one of them later wrote, 'against every form of injustice which either law or custom sanctioned'. They sponsored 'that patent Christianity which', quipped the Rev Sydney Smith, 'has been for some time manufacturing at Clapham to the prejudice of the old admirable article prepared by the Church'. In a later age they would have been agnostic or atheist Fabian Socialists; some of their descendants were.

In this Clapham forcing house Thomas 'talked printed words' when he was four, and at eight wrote an epic on Olaus the Great of Norway, a universal history from the Creation to 1800, and hymns innumerable. He had phenomenal powers of assimilation and memory: 'He seemed to read through the skin', said one observer. He read more quickly than others skimmed, and skimmed as fast as others could turn the pages. He thirsted for knowledge, and if he had not talked and written from his earliest years, 'he would have burst'; his intellect, he afterwards thought, was likely 'to absorb the whole man'.

His parents wisely did not encourage his precocity. They

sent him to a private school in Clapham and later to an Evangelical boarding school, Aspenden Hall in Hertfordshire. There he suffered home sickness for his mother—'the sound of your voice, the touch of your hand'. Another humanising influence on the precocious child were regular holiday visits to his mother's friend, the celebrated Hannah More, one of Dr Johnson's circle, where he was taught to cook and allowed to preach to people brought in from the fields. So the light-haired, rather slight boy remained, for all his erudition, 'playful as a kitten', sweet-tempered, the perfect elder brother arranging games and in the holidays leading expeditions across the Common.

He went to Cambridge in his eighteenth year and the university became the love of his life, exceeded only by his devotion to his young brothers and sisters. His college, Trinity, was to him as Athens to an exiled Greek, and as often as he could in later life he returned to walk the flagged pathway between his rooms and the wall of the chapel, where in the morning of his days he had strolled conning his books. Clever as he was, he found the curriculum hard. There was the tiresome business of the necessary mathematical tripos: 'Oh!', he wrote to his mother, 'for words to express my abomination of that science, . . . I feel myself becoming a personification of Algebra, a living trigonometrical canon, a walking table of logarithms. The pursuit contemptible, below contempt, or disgusting beyond abhorrence. Oh, to change Cam for Isis!' (Oxford made no such demands on its classical aspirants). And, he added, 'All my perceptions of elegance and beauty gone, or at least going'.

There were compensations. He won two Chancellor's gold medals for poetry, a prize for Latin declamation, a Craven classical scholarship and, at a second attempt, a Fellowship, the most desirable honour, in his eyes, that Cambridge had to give, bringing with it £210 a year for seven years, six dozen audit[1] ales at Christmas, a loaf and two pats of butter every morning and a good dinner at High Table for nothing, with almonds and raisins ad lib. at dessert.

What, however, he prized no less were the opportunities to talk to such forgotten luminaries as Moultrie and Charles

[1]An ale of special quality brewed by the University

Austin and Lord Belper and to spout at the Cambridge Union before Coleridge's son, Derwent, and the witty poet and later M.P., W. M. Praed, who thus described the voluble young Macaulay:

Then the favourite comes with his trumpet and drums,
And his arms and his metaphors crossed.

(Zachary was later to complain of his son's *lèse-majesté* in addressing a gathering attended by a Royal Duke with his arms crossed).

Macaulay loved conversation at any hour of the day or night and engaged in it so long as a door was open or a light burning, supping at midnight on milk-punch and roast turkey, drinking tea in floods at three in the morning, pouring out with friends into the dawn and the twittering of birds to chatter down the Madingley Road, debating and debating and learning the 'skill of fence'—Trevelyan's words, —'which rendered him the most redoubtable of antagonists'. That, in the days of the 'Bucks' and the Regency, seems to have been the limit of his roistering. There is no record of any drunkenness or debauchery, when both were commonplace. Macaulay had the purposeful drive of the Victorians, even before the Queen came to the throne.

After Cambridge, he was called to the bar in 1826 and practised desultorily on the Northern circuit. He wrote light verses and other pieces for *Knight's Quarterly Magazine*, and then came a powerful piece on slavery in the West Indies followed by an essay on Milton in the August, 1825, number of the Whig periodical, the *Edinburgh Review*, founded in 1802 and edited by Francis Jeffrey. The effect of this essay, which Macaulay himself later thought 'gaudy and ungraceful', was astonishing: 'Where', asked Jeffrey, 'did you pick up that style?' Overnight he became a celebrity, and invitations to dine fell like confetti on the family breakfast table. Such instant fame from a literary essay, even though it had political connotations, is scarcely credible today.

Reviews such as the *Edinburgh*, the *Quarterly* and *Blackwood's* had, however, great prestige in the early nineteenth century. They existed to satisfy the 'irrepressible passion for discussion' of a small, well-educated, influential public, deprived for so long of an open forum because of the censorship necessitated by the war against France and against French revolutionary ideas. The reviews offered 'talking points' not only about politics but about the national heritage of the arts, history and the law. The leisured classes enjoyed ideas as they enjoyed good food and wines, sport and music, dining out and, for the men, nights at the club.

The *Edinburgh*, for which Macaulay wrote throughout his middle years, was not exclusively Whig: Walter Scott, soundest of Tories, and Robert Southey, a Whig apostate, frequently put life into its often flat and shallow contents. It was, however, Macaulay's brilliant virtuosity that made the *Edinburgh* a *vade mecum* for society, procured him a Commissionership in Bankruptcy at £250 a year, and in 1830 election as M.P. for the Whig Lord Lansdowne's 'pocket' borough[1] of Calne in Wiltshire. Fortunate as always, Macaulay was just in time to profit from the unreformed franchise, into whose coffin he put a few nails, and then benefited from its demise.

On 5 April 1830, he made his maiden speech in a parliament led by the Duke of Wellington in support of a Bill to remove Jewish political disabilities. Across the hurly-burly of the years 1830–32, when England rioted and nine farm labourers were hanged and others transported and the middle classes threatened a run on the banks to bring the Government to heel, Macaulay's shrill, alto voice, monotonous in tone, his words clipped and hissing, poured forth tumultuously in a House of Commons, where parties had splintered into caves and factions and schisms, coteries and cliques. Once on his feet, he stopped neither for breath nor for thought, 'hauling the subject after him with the strength of a giant, till the hearer is left prostrate and powerless by the whirlwind of ideas and emotions that has swept over him', wrote a reporter, G. H. Francis. The extraordinary thing was that the toneless, breathless Macaulay had every listener on tiptoe, not least when he spoke in support of the Whig Reform bills, whose passage raised storms inside and outside Parliament in these years.

Macaulay, adulated at Holland House, adored in his

[1]A Parliamentary seat under the control of one person or family

family circle even though checked by his father, loved the good fellowship and easy equality of the Commons, that best of all clubs, and loved too walking home by daylight after a twelve hour debate. But money became a problem. His commissionership was swept away and his father's firm of Macaulay and Babington, trading with Africa, suffered severe reverses. Macaulay was reduced to selling the gold medals won at Cambridge.

With a fortunate man, all things are fortunate, wrote Theocritus[1], and the advent of Earl Grey's government enabled Macaulay to become the legal member on the Indian Board of Control. In 1834 he accepted a seat on the Supreme Council of India and a salary of a munificent £10,000 a year, out of which he believed he could save £30,000 in five years. He had no desire to go to India; he sacrificed a promising political career simply to 'save my family', to ensure that after a few years they would all be together again, 'in a comfortable though modest, home; certain of a good fire, a good joint of meat, and a good glass of wine'.

The wrench was poignant. Although his mother, that 'bright half of human nature', had died in 1831, his brothers and sisters remained the core of his emotional existence, for he never married. Could he live, exiled, without them? His grief was intense when a sister married and set up house on her own: 'she is dead to me', he wrote. He appealed to his sister Hannah: 'If you will go with me, I will love you better than I love you now, if I can. Whether the period of my exile shall be one of comfort—and after the first shock, even of happiness—depends on you'.

Hannah consented and, with joy now, he set about assembling books—'the *Orlando* in Italian, *Don Quixote* in Spanish, Homer in Greek. . . .'—for the voyage, and finding a lady's maid for Hannah. After three months at sea, they landed at Madras to a 15-gun salute on 10 June 1834 and he wonderingly notes: 'The dark faces, with white turbans, and flowing robes: the trees not our trees: the very smell of the atmosphere that of a hothouse. . . .' He soon met one of the dotty Englishmen who even then haunted British possessions

[1]Ἐν ολβίῳ ὄλβια πάντα

12

overseas. At the British Residency in Mysore, 'I found an Englishman, who, without any preface, accosted me thus: "Pray, Mr Macaulay, do not you think that Buonaparte was the Beast?" "No, Sir, I cannot say that I do". "Sir, he was the Beast, I can prove it. I have found the number 666 in his name. Why, Sir, if he was not the Beast, who was?" "This was a puzzling question, and I am not a little vain of my answer." "Sir," said I, "the House of Commons is the Beast. There are 658 members of the House; and these, with their chief officers—the three clerks, the Sergeant and his deputy, the Chaplain, the doorkeeper, and the librarian,—make 666".'

From India, Macaulay persuaded governments, under Peel and then Melbourne, that censorship should be lifted from the Press, and that English residents should lose the privilege of bringing civil appeals before the Calcutta Supreme Court, thus making natives and English equal before the law. The former relaxation laid him open to the vilest calumnies on account of the latter; the mildest of the local periodicals called him cheat, swindler and charlatan; the others went so much further that he removed the papers from his sister's sitting-room. He himself laughed and stood his ground: 'We were enemies of freedom because we would not suffer a small white aristocracy to domineer over millions.' India could not have a free government, but at least she should have 'a firm and impartial despotism'.

Much more controversial was his support for teaching Indians in English in the higher branches of learning rather than, as previously, in Sanskrit, Arabic and Persian. In the past, Warren Hastings no less than Burke and after him Disraeli, believed that a true liberalism would encourage Indians to study their own no small store of literature, laws, religions and philosophy. Macaulay, in a famous minute, brusquely dismissed all oriental learning: 'There are no books on any subject which deserve to be compared to our own . . . medical doctrines which would disgrace an English farrier, astronomy which would move laughter in the girls at an English boarding-school—history abounding with kings thirty feet high, and reigns 30,000 years long—and geography made up of seas of treacle and seas of butter. . . . I doubt whether the Sanskrit literature be as valuable as that of our Saxon and Norman progenitors'.

Such 'pistolling ways', as Saintsbury called them, so sweeping a dismissal of the Orient and all that in it lay, was wrong. No wonder that Melbourne was once heard to mutter: 'I wish I was as cocksure of any one thing as Macaulay is of everything', or that T. S. Eliot should assert that 'The benefits of British rule will soon be lost, but the ill-effects of the disturbance of a native culture by an alien one will remain'.

Macaulay, however, was possibly right. If Indians were to take responsible positions in the administration—which Macaulay did not doubt would eventually become an Indian administration—English and westernization were essential. English was increasingly the language of commerce throughout the East; neither science nor technology could be understood without it. Just as the languages of Western Europe had civilized Russia in no more than 120 years, so 'I cannot doubt that they will do for the Hindoo what they have done for the Tartar'. So, to a point and a century and half later, they have.

The new edict, announced by Governor-General Sir William Bentinck on 7 March 1835, was that 'the great object of the British Government ought to be the promotion of European literature and science among the natives of India'. Macaulay, as President of the Committee of Public Instruction, set about implementing it, though with an agreeable lack of pomp and purism. Forget logic and rhetoric, he advised: 'Give a boy *Robinson Crusoe*. *Jack the Giant-killer* is better than any book of logic ever written. How ridiculous, he observed, to see Portia represented by a little black boy, or at a school speechday a boy repeating 'some blackguard doggerel of George Colman's, about a fat gentleman who was put to bed over an oven. . . . Really, if we can find nothing better worth reciting than this trash, we had better give up English instruction altogether'.

Allowing himself little respite even in the rainy season when most of his colleagues fell sick, Macaulay drafted a code for criminal law which was later adopted and is still the basis, however eroded, of Indian law. He found time for vast reading from Hesiod to Macrobius in the 'long, languid leisure of the Calcutta afternoon, while the punkah swung overhead, and the air came heavy and scented through the moistened grass-matting which shrouded the windows'. He disliked formal banquets and 'the most deplorable twaddle' there to be heard. Like Gibbon, he had a poor opinion of parsons; when others worked, 'the reverend gentlemen are always within doors in the heat of the day, lying on their backs, regretting breakfast, longing for tiffin, and crying out for lemonade'. He thought little of native Indian fruits ('a plantain is very like a rotten pear . . . a yam is an indifferent potato').

Always, he longed to be in England, pining (to adapt his own poem on the old Jacobite), by the Hooghly for his 'lovelier' Thames. When Hannah married Charles Trevelyan, Macaulay suffered a 'frightening' mental disturbance. It passed and he left India, never to return, in 1838. The Trevelyans went with him, and on board ship he nursed their baby daughter an hour or so a day and taught her to talk.

Back in London, work on his long-projected *History*, then visualised as extending from the Revolution of 1688 to the death of George IV in 1830, was postponed. Macaulay was elected an M.P. for Edinburgh and Melbourne called him to be Secretary-at-War and a member of the Cabinet. He was not yet forty. *The Times*, snobbishly averse from the elevation of such a middle-class person, referred to him as 'Mr Babbletongue Macaulay'. In cabinet, with his rumpled appearance, strange eyes and 'waterspouts of talk', he was regarded as an oddity, Melbourne remarking that he would prefer to sit in 'a room with a chime of bells, ten parrots and Lady Westmorland' than with Macaulay.

His new post was easy. 'The House of Commons of 1840 spent upon the Army very little of its own time, or of the nation's money', his nephew wrote. Macaulay had, however, to defend the notorious Earl of Cardigan, who by purchase commanded a fine cavalry regiment, the 11th Hussars, which he proceeded, as Trevelyan puts it, to 'drag through a slough of scandal, favouritism, petty tyranny and intrigue', duelling with a lieutenant and flogging a soldier on a Sunday between church services. With his customary skill, Macaulay resisted demands for Cardigan's removal from his command, thus leaving him free to quarrel fifteen years later in the Crimea with his brother-in-law, Lord Lucan, and to lead the charge of the Light Brigade into the valley of death.

Macaulay, longing for 'liberty and ease, freedom of speech and freedom of pen', had not long to wait. The Whigs resigned in August 1841. 'Now I am free. I am independent', he wrote to Napier, Jeffrey's successor at the *Edinburgh*. 'I am in Parliament, as honourably seated as a man can be. My family is comfortably off. I have leisure for literature . . . I am sincerely and thoroughly contented'. He was to have one more brief spell in office as Paymaster-General in Lord John Russell's Cabinet. With a break of five years, he remained M.P. for Edinburgh until 1856.

From 1841 Macaulay was nearly a full-time writer. In 1842 appeared his only major poetic collection, *The Lays of Ancient Rome*, a sweeping success, and soon into a second edition. Next year came the first authorized edition of his *Critical and Historical Essays* with no less success. Not surprisingly perhaps it was Macaulay, the M.P., who occupied himself with extending the copyright protection on books from 28 to 42 years from the date of publication; his bill passed to the statute book.

His letters, at present being published *in toto*[1], to his great friend Ellis and to his sisters are delightful. Taking a holiday from his labours on his *History*, he set out in 1843 for a tour of the Loire, via a train to Brighton: slow, crowded, he tells Hannah, with 'a sick lady smelling of aether; a healthy gentleman smelling of brandy; the thermometer at 102 degrees in the shade and I not in the shade'.

With his nephew and nieces he happily dawdled hours away, inventing games and small dramas for them, himself playing a dog-stealer or Dando, the clown, at an oyster-shop, and he wrote small poems for them to recite.

> There once was a nice little girl,
>   With a nice little rosy face.
> She always said 'Our Father',
>   And she always said her grace.

[1] See entry in the bibliography, p 58

He took the children on tours of London to the Zoo, and to Mme Tussaud's; he hired a whole railway compartment for a trip to York and Cambridge and once even to Paris. 'How such things twine themselves about our hearts!', he wrote. Travelling was also necessary for his *History*. As Thackeray said: 'he travels a hundred miles to make a line of description', here sketching the ground-plan of streets, there timing how long it took to walk round town walls. When he wandered alone through Whitehall or down by the old houses near the river, he invented conversations between the great people of past times. In the country he usually read as he walked. One afternoon he re-read the last five books of the *Iliad* and had to turn aside from a party of walkers lest they 'should see me blubbering for imaginary beings, the creations of a ballad-maker who has been dead 2,700 years'.

This eccentric, stumpy figure—a book in breeches, Sydney Smith called him—still loved good talk, especially at the social breakfasts, then all the vogue, where verse was declaimed, memory tested, and repartee sparkled between such as Sydney Smith, Hallam, Greville, Hobhouse and such Lords as Carlisle, Lansdowne and Mahon. Bolt upright in his chair, hands folded over the handle of his walking stick, Macaulay brightened 'from the forehead downwards when a burst of humour was coming'. Now he seldom talked to win; 'truly considerate towards others—so delicately courteous'. Carlyle saw in his face in repose as he was reading—'homely Norse features that you find everywhere in the Western Isles . . . an honest good sort of fellow, made out of oatmeal'. To another observer: 'his was the sort of face you might expect above a cobbler's apron'.

After protracted labours, rewriting, reading aloud, punctilious proof correction, and author's twitch—'I see everyday more clearly how my performance is below excellence'—the first two volumes of the *History* appeared in December 1848, to be greeted by what his biographer called 'an ebullition of national pride and satisfaction'. Daily his publisher, Longman, brought him 'triumphant bulletins'. The first edition of 3,000 was sold within ten days; the third by the end of January 1849. By April 1850 22,000 copies had gone. 'I feel no intoxicating effect', he noted in his

Journal, 'but a man may be drunk without knowing it'. Walking past a bookshop window he saw David Hume's famous *History of England* advertised as 'valuable as an introduction to Macaulay' and laughed 'so convulsively' that he was taken 'for a poor demented gentleman'.

He became Rector of Glasgow University; he was offered the Cambridge Professorship of modern history by Prince Albert and he stayed at Windsor: 'When we went into the drawing-room, the Queen came to me with great animation, and insisted on my telling her some of my stories, which she had heard at second-hand from George Grey. I certainly made her laugh heartily. She talked on for some time, most courteously and pleasantly'.

His affluence made him royally, if not always discriminatingly, generous. He lived now in a fine villa on Campden Hill, kept four servants and 'set up' his own brougham in which he drove, 'pleased and proud'. Did he ever pass the fine house in Regent's Terrace, where the wealthy Engels was plotting the downfall of England? Certainly when he visited the Exhibition of 1851 in Hyde Park, he 'saw none of the men of action with whom the Socialists were threatening us'. But he was exhilarated by 'the boats and little frigates darting across the lake, the flags, the music, the guns'. Paxton's building 'a most gorgeous sight; vast, graceful, beyond the dreams of the Arabian romances. . . . I was quite dazzled and felt as I did on entering St Peter's'. He revelled in the ingenuity of his times.

Next year, however, illness struck him and Bright, the physician, told him the action of his heart was deranged. He was never quite well again, suffering from bronchitis and asthma and fits of violent coughing. He contemplated his final end with 'perfect serenity', regretting only the leaving those he loved, and declared that he was growing 'happier and happier'. Six years, however, were left him and he husbanded his powers to finish the next two volumes of his *History*. Despite days when he felt impotent and despondent, he delighted in 'a work which never presses and never ceases'.

Volumes three and four appeared in December, 1855, in an edition of 25,000 copies weighing, he noted, 56 tons.

Their success was enormous and they were translated into nearly all European languages as well as Persian. In 1857 he became, to universal acclaim, a baron; and in 1858 paid a last visit to Cambridge when—though scarcely able to totter across Clare Bridge—he was made High Steward of the borough.

Though he tried to continue his *History*, he found it hard to settle to work and in his heart knew he would not complete even his volume on Queen Anne's reign. He died without pain in his library, fully dressed and seated in his easy chair on 28 December 1859. He was buried, like his father, in Westminster Abbey.

II. POLITICS

Macaulay's introduction to practical politics was a cat flung into his face during an election meeting at Cambridge. At Leicester, when he was twenty-six, he worked for a Whig candidate and had to be dissuaded from rushing out to confront the mob, 128 of whom ended up in gaol after the yeomanry were called out. Campaigning for himself in newly-enfranchised Leeds, he fled from the threat of physical attack when his opponents climbed on to the roof of the coach where he was addressing a drunken, disorderly crowd; and he allowed himself to refer to his Tory opponent as a 'hyena', in return no doubt for being dubbed 'an impertinent puppy' by *Blackwood's*.

He was, he said, in 1839 a Whig because that party had established 'our civil and religious liberties'.

to the Whigs of the seventeenth century we owe it that we have a House of Commons. To the Whigs of the nineteenth century we owe it that the House of Commons has been purified. The abolition of the slave trade, the abolition of colonial slavery, the extension of popular education, the mitigation of the rigour of the penal code, all, all were effected by that party; and of that party, I repeat, I am a member.

19

As for the future, the party

should leave themselves (the public) to their own legitimate duties—by leaving capital to find its most lucrative course, commodities their fair prices, industry and intelligence their natural reward, idleness and folly their natural punishment—by maintaining peace, by defending property, by diminishing the price of law, and by observing strict economy in every department of the state. Let the Government do this—the People will assuredly do the rest.

But what *was* the Whig party of which he was determined to remain a member? In the late 1820s and 1830s, it was as amoebic a thing as the Tory party, all protoplasmic limbs forever waving out to touch and link and unlink with neighbouring limbs. Ultra-Tories joined some Whigs in demanding the Parliamentary reform which most Tories opposed; Canning, the Tory, supported liberalising movements abroad as did Peel at home; and Brougham, the Whig, sought to fuse his aristocratic, land-owning party with the Tory commercial classes. Macaulay's political position reflected the amorphous condition of the politics of his time.

He spoke notably in favour of Catholic emancipation, that is to allow them to sit in Parliament and, to the same end, for the Jews. A Jew could own half London, but could not sit in the Commons—ludicrous! With great force he supported the Reform bills of 1831–32, the burden of his argument being that if the franchise was not expanded, there would be revolution:

Turn where we may, within, around, the voice of great events is proclaiming to us, Reform, that you may preserve. Now, therefore, while everything at home and abroad forebodes ruin to those who persist in a hopeless struggle against the spirit of the age, now, while the crash of the proudest throne of the continent is still resounding in our ears, now, while the roof of a British palace affords an ignominious shelter to the exiled heir of forty kings, now, while we see on every side ancient institutions subverted, and great societies dissolved, now, while the heart of England is still sound, now, while old feelings and old associations retain a power and a charm which may too soon pass away, now, in this your accepted time, now, in this your day of salvation, take counsel, not of prejudice, not of party spirit, not of the ignominious pride of a fatal consistency, but of history, of reason, of the ages which are past, of the signs of this most portentous time. Pronounce in a manner worthy of the expectation with which this great debate has been anticipated, and of the long remembrance which it will leave behind. Renew the youth of the State. Save property, divided against itself. Save the multitude, endangered by its own unpopular power. Save the greatest, and fairest, and most highly civilised community that ever existed, from calamities which may in a few days sweep away all the rich heritage of so many ages of wisdom and glory. The danger is terrible. The time is short. If this bill should be rejected, I pray to God that none of those who concur in rejecting it may ever remember their votes with unavailing remorse, amidst the wreck of laws, the confusion of ranks, the spoliation of property, and the dissolution of social order!

Whether Macaulay's speeches affected the issue is debatable. The bills passed in the end because one party leader thought it desirable and the other found it expedient. The Acts were more sweeping than is sometimes supposed: a quarter of the borough seats were wiped out, some great industrial centres were enfranchised, even though only for those occupying houses whose rentable value was £10 or over a year, and even though the vote in the counties was still confined to the forty shilling freeholders. This was quite enough for Macaulay. No more concessions; 'My firm conviction is that, in our country, universal suffrage is incompatible, not with this or that form of Government, but with all forms of Government, and with everything for the sake of which forms of Government exist; that is, incompatible with property and that is consequently incompatible with civilization'.

He shared the Radicals' distaste for aristocratic privilege and pretentiousness. He shared the Tory and moderate Whig fears that with universal suffrage, the majority of voters would be poor and ignorant people whose interest, at least in the short term, which is all they would visualize, would be to plunder the rich, whether through taxes, confiscation, or otherwise. (Effectively this has come about in the twentieth century). This majority 'if they have the power, will commit waste of every sort on the estate of man-

kind and'—here he talks in the very accent of Burke—
'transmit it to posterity impoverished and desolated'.

He spoke for the middle ranks, 'that brave, honest and
sound-hearted class', who knew that wealth must be accumulated and that democracy would annihilate capital, and
reduce the most flourishing countries to 'the state of Barbary
or the Morea'. He laughed off the mouthings of 'this small
sect of Utilitarians', who demanded votes for all. 'Though
quibbling about self-interest and motives, and objects of
desire, and the greatest happiness of the greatest number, is
but a poor employment for a grown man, it certainly hurts
the health less than hard drinking, and the fortune less than
high play: it is not much more laughable than phrenology,
and is immeasurably more humane than cock-fighting'.

Macaulay was early and late against 'one man, one vote'.
In 1857—two years before he died—he wrote to H. S.
Randall: 'I have long been convinced that institutions purely
democratic must, sooner or later, destroy liberty or civilization, or both. In Europe, where the population is dense, the
effect of such institutions would be almost instantaneous.
. . . Either the poor would plunder the rich and civilization
would perish; or order and prosperity would be saved by a
strong military government, and liberty would perish!'.

Randall was the biographer of Jefferson whose country
had adopted universal suffrage. As long as free land was
available, Macaulay told him, there would probably be no
'fatal calamity', but the day will come when in the State of
New York a multitude of people, none of whom has had
more than half a breakfast, or expects to have more than
half a dinner, will choose a Legislature. Is it possible to doubt
what sort of a Legislature will be chosen? . . . There is nothing
to stop you. Your Constitution is all sail and no anchor. . . .
Your Huns and Vandals will have been engendered within
your own country by your own institutions'.

Macaulay, in short, was all for liberty and against equality,
which he knew could not exist. But there was a dilemma.
It was fatal, he thought, to trust unpropertied masses with
political power; yet the very industrialization, mechanization
and urban development he admired created wealth, and
wealth set off a vast increase in population, a greater inequality

in income and, thus, the danger of explosive mobs. He pictured vividly for M.P.s the Gordon 'No Popery' riots of 1780, proof of the proposition 'that the ignorance of the common people makes the property, the limbs, the lives of all classes insecure'. These swollen mobs were not of the past only. Over the years they had caused 'the riots of Nottingham, the sack of Bristol, all the outrages of Ludd,[1] and Swing, and Rebecca, beautiful and costly machinery broken to pieces in Yorkshire, barns and haystacks blazing in Kent, fences and buildings pulled down in Wales'.

Yet it was that 'beautiful and costly machinery' which could bring a better future.

If we were to prophesy that in the year 1930 a population of fifty millions, better fed, clad, and lodged than the English of our time, will cover these islands; that Sussex and Huntingdonshire will be wealthier than the wealthiest parts of the West Riding of Yorkshire now are; that cultivation, rich as that of a flower-garden, will be carried up to the very tops of Ben Nevis and Helvellyn; that machines constructed on principles yet undiscovered will be in every house; that there will be no highways but railroad, no travelling but by steam; that our debt, vast as it seems to us, will appear to our grandchildren a trifling encumbrance which might easily be paid off in a year or two—many people would think us insane.

For all his anti-Radicalism, his vision here is as materialistic as that of the Utilitarians and he is not far away from the Benthamite calculus. He thoroughly approved 'the Baconian doctrine, Utility and Progress', and with almost Marxist scorn dismisses any other considerations: 'Shoes have kept villains from being wet; we doubt whether Seneca ever kept anybody from being angry'. This is to dismiss morality in favour of materialism.

---

[1]The Luddite riots took place in Nottinghamshire in 1811 and were directed against the introduction of machinery into the textile industry which caused the dismissal of many craftsmen. Swing was a fictitious Captain in whose name intimidating letters were sent to farmers and landowners in Southern England during 1830-31 and their ricks set on fire. The Rebecca riots took place in South Wales in 1843 in protest against the charges levied at toll gates on the public roads, the rioters being mounted and disguised as women. Macaulay's speech was made in 1847.

How then to stop the mob from wrecking the future from which they had most to gain? The answer must be: to educate them. Macaulay strongly supported the Government's request in 1847 for a grant of £100,000 for the education of those who could not afford to pay for it for their children. It was the only possible way to avoid the ignorance of the 'common people', which was the 'principal cause of danger to our property and persons'; the alternative was 'guns and bayonets, stocks and whipping posts, treadmills, solitary cells, penal colonies, gibbets'. Make men 'better and wiser and happier', or make them 'infamous and miserable'. Obviously we must prevent 'hundreds and thousands of our countrymen from becoming mere Yahoos'. Through education, the poor man might be persuaded to 'find pleasure in the exercise of his intellect, be taught to revere his maker, taught to respect legitimate authority, and taught at the same time to seek the redress of real wrongs by peaceful means'.

Macaulay does not ask with Socrates, whether in fact virtue can be taught, nor wonder whether schooling can compensate for social ills. Moreover, a little learning often merely makes mobs craftier, and itself may become the instrument of a subversiveness which is far more dangerous to 'property and persons' than the irrationality of mobs. 'A proletariat', writes Russell Kirk with the benefit of hindsight, 'does not cease to be proletarian because it has been compelled to drowse through state schools—or because the price of corn has decreased five shillings a quarter'.

Macaulay's support for State financing of education landed him in the same camp where the Radicals jostled ultra-Tory paternalists such as Southey. Macaulay had condemned both and was generally against State intervention. The State might be allowed to erect buildings for public purposes; but that must be the end of it. Free, private enterprise was essential: 'We firmly believe that £500,000 subscribed by individuals for railroads or canals would produce more advantage to the public than five millions voted by Parliament for the same purpose'.

His position was self-contradictory and made him uneasy. He spoke on 29 April 1846, about a bill to limit the labour of young persons in factories to ten hours a day. The argument against it was that it concerned 'one of those matters which settle themselves far better than any Government can settle them'. This normally would have been his own standpoint, particularly where factory owners whom he respected and to whom he bore goodwill, were involved. But he saw the dilemma:

I hardly know which is the greater pest to society, a paternal government, that is to say a prying, meddlesome government, which intrudes itself into every part of human life, and which thinks that it can do everything for everybody better than anybody can do anything for himself; or a careless, lounging government, which suffers grievances, such as it could at once remove, to grow and multiply, and which to all complaint and remonstrance has only one answer: 'We must let things alone: we must let things take their course: we must let things find their level.' There is no more important problem in politics than to ascertain the just mean between these two most pernicious extremes, to draw correctly the line which divides those cases in which it is the duty of the State to interfere from those cases in which it is the duty of the State to abstain from interference.

Difficult indeed! We certainly do not want to go back, he ruminates, to rulers in 'the old time', who were always telling people 'how to keep their shops, how to till their fields, how to educate their children, how many dishes to have on their tables, how much a yard to give for the cloth which made their coats'. Such rulers were 'so much shocked by the cunning and hardheartedness of moneylenders that they made laws against usury; and the consequence was that the borrower, who, if he had been left unprotected, would have got money at ten per cent . . . could hardly, when protected, get it at fifteen per cent!'.

Macaulay declares himself strongly attached to the 'principle of free trade', and to non-interference with it 'on commercial grounds'. Yet, he claims, we rightly interfere with trade for the sake of national defence; we fix rates of pay for cabs plying for hire; we forbid farmers to cultivate tobacco. We stop trade in 'licentious books and pictures' on the grounds of morality; we may order a man to build a drain to an old house on the grounds of public health'.

Reluctantly, he concludes that we *should* restrict working hours, for who can 'doubt that twelve hours a day of labour in a factory is too much for a lad of thirteen?'.

Moreover, with such hours there could be no leisure, and without leisure there could be no time for his pet panacea, education. Minors in any case must be protected. No one, he asserts, doubts that we should, for example, prevent a wealthy youth of thirteen from conveyancing his estate or giving a bond of £50,000. The poor minor is no less our concern than the rich one, particularly as the only inheritance of the poor is 'the sound mind in the sound body'. The first Factory Act, introduced by Peel's father in 1802, had had none but beneficial results. Long hours over the year would produce less than shorter ones.

Then again, he reflects, man is more than a 'machine for the production of worsted and calico'; he is 'fearfully and wonderfully made'. Even a fine horse or a sagacious dog is not treated like a spinning jenny; a labourer is no 'mere wheel or pulley!... Treat boys and men so, and England will become 'a feeble and ignoble race, parents of a more feeble and more ignoble progeny'. Our great industrial inventors have usually been from the artisan class—Hargreaves, Crompton; that class must be protected, even if only from the point of view of national self-interest:

Never will I believe that what makes a population stronger, and healthier, and wiser, and better, can ultimately make it poorer. You try to frighten us by telling us that, in some German factories, the young work seventeen hours in the twenty-four, that they work so hard that among thousands there is not one who grows to such a stature that he can be admitted into the army; and you ask whether, if we pass this bill, we can possibly hold our own against such competition as this? Sir, I laugh at the thought of such competition. If ever we are forced to yield the foremost place among commercial nations, we shall yield it, not to a race of degenerate dwarfs, but to some people pre-eminently vigorous in body and mind.

Macaulay sums up with his customary antitheses and the help of the Prayer Book:

We have regulated that which we should have left to regulate itself. We have left unregulated that which we were bound to regulate. We have given to some branches of industry a protection which has proved their bane. We have withheld from public health and public morals the protection which was their due. We have prevented the labourer from buying his loaf where he could get it cheapest; but we have not prevented him from ruining his body and mind by premature and immoderate toil. I hope that we have seen the last both of a vicious system in interference and of a vicious system of non-interference, and that our poorer country-men will no longer have reason to attribute their sufferings either to our meddling or to our neglect.

His speeches in the Commons, however splutteringly delivered, riveted his hearers so that they did not notice their repetitiousness. His speech on the Anatomy Bill, as G. M. Young pointed out, has only two central points; the poor are most in danger of burking (i.e. of the body-snatcher) and the poor are the greatest sufferers from bad surgery. Each is restated six times, and the demonstration is rounded off with a picturesque anecdote. But in the course of the short speech Macaulay has touched on the habits of murderers in various countries, the Russian peasants and the Czar, mountebanks and barbers, old women and charms, the squaring of the circle and the transit of Venus, Richard of England, Leopold of Austria, and the bricklayer who falls from a ladder. The matter is perfectly fused, the speed exhilarating, and he ends before the listener has rightly discerned where he is going.

His phrasing was often memorable and could sting: Radicals 'without talents or acquirements sufficient for the management of a vestry', he said, 'sometimes become dangerous to great empires'. Some of his *trouvailles* have become part of the language: 'The gallery in which the reporters sit', he was the first to remark, 'has become the fourth estate of the realm'. Such apophthegms, which are everywhere in his *Essays* also, were not the inspiration of the moment. All his speeches were carefully prepared, not however in writing, which he thought detracted from their spontaneity, but in his head and, when perfect, there committed to memory. A good speech, he told his sister Margaret, emerged from plan and order and should sound careless and unconscious.

Macaulay was by all accounts scrupulous in his parliamentary duties and regularly in his seat. To those who elected him he was peremptory and even arrogant, and in those days M.P.s once elected rarely visited their constituencies. They were representatives, not delegates, and Macaulay resented being button-holed by all those who thought they had a right to see him. There were lighter moments. He wrote to his sister: 'Colonel Torrens made a tipsy speech about rents and profits, and then staggered away, tumbled down a stairway and was sick as a dog in the Long Gallery'.

Through all Macaulay's political thought runs an underlying pragmatism, more typical of the Whigs than of the Radicals and Tories: 'I rest my opinion on no general theory of government. I distrust all general theories of government', he once told the Commons, and he praised the leadership of 'practical statesmen'. It was practical to reform the franchise; impractical (and dangerous) to create a universal franchise. Reform, however, was not merely an *ad hoc* necessity; it was, on his reading of history, an historical necessity too: 'The Great Charters, the assembling of the first House of Commons, the Petition of Right, the Declaration of Right, the Bill now on our table, what are they all but steps in one great progress?'. A progress led, of course, by Whigs with their idea of government as 'a progressive science'. Tories had merely followed on: 'the tail is now where the head was some generations ago'; he agreed that a Queen Anne Tory is a modern Whig.

He himself, he always insisted, was a Whig not a Liberal; he smote Bentham for his ideas of 'planning', which he at once detected as being illiberal and, if pushed, tyrannical. 'You call me a Liberal', he once said, 'but I don't know that in these days I deserve the name. I am opposed to the abolition of standing armies. I am opposed to the abrogation of capital punishment. I am opposed to the destruction of the National Church. In short, I am in favour of wars, hanging, and Church Establishment'.

He was a patriotic Englishman, deeply concerned about national defence; towards the end of his life, he read with concentration of every move in the war with Russia in the

Crimea. He came to be at one with the Whig Burke's philosophy of conservatism.

III. ESSAYS

Political concepts also run through the essays he regularly wrote for the *Edinburgh Review*, but they are not the reason why the public gobbled up edition after edition of his selection of them, *Critical and Historical Essays*, published in 1842. Such early essays as 'The West Indies' and 'Milton' (1825), with their forceful Whiggism, appealed to those involved in politics; his firm and optimistic belief that England had progressed and would continue to do so was welcome to an age flexing its industrial and technological muscles. Few would deny the commendation of the Reform Acts implied in his essay on 'Mirabeau' (1832), where he wrote that the French aristocracy 'would not have reform and they had revolution. They would not endure Turgot and they were forced to endure Robespierre'.

These observations were acceptable. What was irresistible, and to an ever-widening public, was his vivid, swift narration of men's lives or of historical happenings. His analyses of literary and philosophical works and of complex situations were crystal clear; he never wrote an obscure sentence; he seemed to get to the heart of every matter. His phrases were a joy; his iconoclasm challenging; his reasoning persuasive and he soon had his readers convinced that what he thought they had long thought though, admittedly, 'ne'er so well expressed'.

He etched on to the minds of generations of Victorian and Edwardian readers pictures that would last their lifetimes—of the blind Milton in his small lodging sitting at the old organ beneath the faded green hangings, 'the quick twinkle of his eyes, rolling in vain to find the day'; of Byron's 'so sad and dark a story', condemned by 'the British public in one of its periodical fits of morality'; of Bacon, weak in character, powerful in mind, whose 'humble aim' in his philosophy was 'to make imperfect men comfortable'; of Warren

Hastings' great qualities, though 'to represent him as a man of stainless virtue is to make him ridiculous'.

If they recalled anything of the war of the Spanish Succession, or Machiavelli, or Horace Walpole, or the then unperformed playwrights of the Restoration, they recalled Macaulay's colourful and cogent representations of them; and it is not too much to say that their stock of general knowledge came to a great extent from that 'vast mine, rich with a hundred ores' which Macaulay ascribes to Addison, but which more fittingly applies to his own lavishly stocked mind.

Immaterial to them—and to us—the numerous refutations of Macaulay's facts, deductions and dramatic *scenas;* immaterial, too, such criticism as De Quincey's, 'Every sentence seems saturated with its separate charge of quicksilver; and paragraph after paragraph roll off in volleys of minute explosions, flashes, raps, and bounces, like the small artillery of a schoolboy, or the *feu-de-joie* of squibs'—immaterial because this is exactly what readers loved.

Click goes Macaulay's camera, and we see amid the admirers of Fanny Burney and her *Evelina*, Burke, Gibbon, Sheridan, one other: the royal Duke of Cumberland who 'acknowledged her merit, after his fashion, by biting his lips and wriggling in his chair whenever her name was mentioned': click again, and here is Madame Schwellenberg, 'a hateful old toadeater', and Doctor Burney himself, an excellent musician and man, who, however, 'thought going to Court like going to Heaven'.

Nevertheless Macaulay gives, too, a just estimate of Fanny Burney's writings and her place in literary history, no less than in the coruscating 'Milton' he calls attention to the prose writings of the poet, then little read, to the sublime 'wisdom' of the *Areopagitica*, to 'the devotional and lyric rapture' of passages which are 'a perfect field of the cloth of gold', by whose side 'the finest declamations of Burke sink into insignificance', and he offers the exquisite comparison of Milton's poetry to 'the roses and myrtles which bloom unchilled on the verge of the avalanche' in the Alps. Bacon may have been a weak man in Macaulay's eyes, but in his *Essay* on him, as in few later studies, he puts a luminous finger on the real originality of the *Novum Organum* and the *Advancement of Learning:* 'The philosophy of Plato began in words and ended in words. . . . The philosophy of Bacon began in observations and ended in arts. . . . An acre in Middlesex is better than a principality in Utopia. The smallest actual good is better than the most magnificent promises of impossibilities'.

Where others used abstractions, he personalized. Socrates and Phaedrus do not merely hold a discussion; they hold it 'on that fine summer day under the plane-tree, while the fountains warbled at their feet, and the cicadas chirped overhead'. He does not refer to the characters in Restoration plays as licentious and libidinous; they have 'foreheads of bronze, hearts like the nether millstone, and tongues set on fire of hell'. Warren Hastings does not take up a clerkship: 'he is immediately placed at a desk in the Secretary's office'. England and France do not become allies; they 'pair off together'. We are not told that Count Orloff, ablaze with medals, is tall, but that he 'brushes the ceiling with his toupee'.

Up into the night sky go the fireworks, the rockets and Roman candles, at once keeping readers from their beds and lighting up Macaulay's often highly original and complex notions on, for example, the contradictory traits in Machiavelli, exalting liberty at the same time as he advocated dissimulation—contradictory only, suggests Macaulay, because of the wide gap in value judgments between northern and southern races. Iago was detested by northern audiences for his wicked plots; an Italian audience might find something to admire in his wit, clarity of mind and skill in dissimulation.

Here Macaulay stands, long before most historians, on the principle of moral relativism, of not judging men of the past by contemporary standards: 'He alone reads history aright, who, observing how powerfully circumstances influence the feelings and opinions of men, how often vices pass into virtues and paradoxes into axioms, learns to distinguish what is accidental and transitory in human nature from what is essential and immutable'. In the end, however, Macaulay kow-tows to the prejudices of his time: yes, *Il Principe* is immoral and offensive.

Although Macaulay sometimes circumspectly shrank away from his own originality, he persisted in it. He, Whig progressive as he was, asserted in his 'Burleigh' essay that the Tudor despotism was popular and no bad thing. They had to take heed of public opinion because they had no means of protecting themselves against public hatred. So public favour had to be courted, which meant that the public of the sixteenth century, while lacking 'the outward show of freedom', had the reality—they were beyond all doubt a free people, and he adds the still-relevant *caveat:* 'Constitutions, charters, petitions of right, declarations of right, representative assemblies, electoral colleges, are not good government; nor do they, even when most elaborately constructed, necessarily produce good government'.

His readers also marvelled at and enjoyed the extraordinary range of his knowledge. They felt they were being agreeably educated when, discussing dramatists, he chatted about Islamism and Brahminism; or, in an essay on a minor poet, he wrote of 'the practices of puffers, a class of people who have more than once talked the public into the most absurd errors', of the age of private patronage when men of letters spent 'their lives in dangling at the heels of the wealthy and power-ful', and when he tossed in, here, a generalization—'Men of real merit will, if they persevere, at last reach the station to which they are entitled'—there an *aperçu* such as that Pope 'kept up the dignity of the literary character so much better' because at thirty he possessed £6–7,000. Yet nowhere is there a sense of his stretching out the long arm. All comes as naturally as can be.

What a variety of arrows did his quiver contain and some of them quite deadly! Of the three-volume life of Burghley by the Oxford Regius Professor of Modern History, Dr. Nares, he writes: 'Compared with the labour of reading through these volumes, all other labour, the labour of thieves on the treadmill, of children in factories, of negroes in sugar plantations, is an agreeable recreation'. He performed another hatchet job on the then popular poet, Robert Montgomery whose writing, says Macaulay, bears the same relation to poetry as a Turkey carpet bears to a picture. Mr. Montgomery he admits, uses words which 'when disposed in certain orders and combinations have made, and will again make, good poetry. But, as they now stand, they seem to be put together on principle in such a manner as to give no image of anything "in the heavens above, or in the earth beneath or in the waters under the earth" '.

His readers wriggled with pleasure when Macaulay deflated a public figure such as the Poet Laureate, Robert Southey, who, from being a republican had turned ultra-Tory. Macaulay begins, smooth as silk, by praising Southey's *Life of Nelson* as 'most perfect and most delightful'. But, oh dear, this new work, 'Sir Thomas More, or Colloquies on the Progress and Prospects of Society' ! Tongue in cheek he gives a *précis* of it. The Laureate is sitting by his fireside reading his newspaper. An elderly person appears whom he takes to be an American gentleman come to stare at the Lakes and the Lake-poets among whom Southey is numbered.

Mr. Southey is, however, mistaken:

The visitor informs the hospitable poet that he is not an American but a spirit. Mr Southey, with more frankness than civility, tells him that he is a very queer one. The stranger holds out his hand. It has neither weight nor substance. Mr Southey upon this becomes more serious; his hair stands on end; and he adjures the spectre to tell him what he is and why he comes. The ghost turns out to be Sir Thomas More. The traces of martyrdom, it seems, are worn in the other world, as stars and ribands are worn in this. Sir Thomas shows the poet a red streak round his neck, brighter than a ruby, and informs him that Cranmer wears a suit of flames in Paradise, the right hand glove, we suppose, of peculiar brilliancy. Sir Thomas pays but a short visit on this occasion, but promises to cultivate the new acquaintance which he has formed, and, after begging that his visit may be kept secret from Mrs Southey, vanishes into air!

If Southey momentarily survived this sardonic raillery, he tottered when Macaulay summed up his political philosophy: 'To stand on a hill, to look at a cottage and a factory, and to see which is prettier', and fell to the floor when Macaulay stigmatised his paternalism as necessitating 'a Lady Bountiful in every parish, a Paul Pry in every house, spying, eavesdropping, relieving, admonishing, spending our money for us, and choosing our opinions for us'. It is ironical that

33

Macaulay's none too scrupulous lampooning of Southey's high Toryism should put us in mind of the Socialism *de nos jours*.

Macaulay could wield the broadsword as well as the poignard. J. W. Croker's edition of a five-volume text of Boswell's Johnson is 'ill compiled, ill arranged, ill written and ill printed'. Croker's notes 'swarm with mis-statements . . . scandalous inaccuracy . . . ignorance, heedlessness . . . classical blunders' for which even a schoolboy would expect a flogging. Croker, Tory M.P. and *Blackwood's* contributor, never forgot an injury: twenty years later he wrote a rancorous review of the first two volumes of Macaulay's *History*.

Macaulay had little time either for Boswell—'thoughtless loquacity'—or for Johnson himself, a shocking anti-Whig whom he portrays as grotesque, uncouth and maladroit. But, observed his sister Margaret, noting her brother's shambling deportment and careless dress, Macaulay and Johnson had similarities: their hatred of cant, their disputatiousness, their indifference to the beauties of nature. And what Macaulay said of Johnson's style was later said, though not quite fairly, of his own. When Johnson spoke, he used simple, energetic and picturesque words, observes Macaulay, but 'when he wrote for publication, he did his sentences out of English into Johnsonese. . . . His letters from the Hebrides to Mrs. Thrale are the original of that work of which the *Journey to the Hebrides* is the translation; and it is amusing to compare the two versions. "When we were taken up stairs", says Johnson in one of his letters, "a dirty fellow bounced out of the bed on which one of us was to lie". This incident is recorded in the *Journey* as follows: "Out of one of the beds on which we were to repose started up, at our entrance, a man black as a Cyclops from the forge" '.

Generally, however, the *Essays* are more appreciative than depreciative. Macaulay's 'Byron' essay, written as early as 1831, gives a sympathetic and understanding account of the 'great literary revolution' brought about by Wordsworth—whose later poems he thought a bore—Coleridge and the rest, and indicates his own predilections firmly: 'We prefer a gipsy by Reynolds to his Majesty's head on a signpost, and a Borderer by Scott to a Senator by Addison'. He praises 'the magnificent imagery and the varied music of Coleridge and Shelley'. He declares that the 'heart of man is the province of poetry, and of poetry alone'. Cowper was the forerunner of 'the great restoration of our literature'—poor, gentle, melancholy Cowper, 'whose spirit' (and here Macaulay sinks into bathos), 'had been broken by fagging at school'. Macaulay recovers to specify what for him was the nature of the 'restoration': 'Instead of raving about imaginary Chloes and Sylvias, Cowper wrote of Mrs. Unwin's knitting needles'. It was the sort of particularizing that Macaulay himself gloried in. But if a lady's knitting needles, why not Simon Lee's 'ankles swollen and thick' or 'Spade! with which Wilkinson hath tilled his lands?' Answer: the ankles and spade were Wordsworth, whom he disliked, not Cowper whom he admired.

Surprisingly, it was Byron who for Macaulay consummated the poetic 'revolution', though he never quite shows how, except in a rather irrelevant witticism alleging that Byron, who lived much abroad, founded 'an exoteric Lake school'. What indeed had the musing Wordsworth and the drug-inspired Coleridge to do with the Regency Byron and his fans who discarded their neckcloths in imitation of him, practised at the mirror the curl of the lip and the scowl, and many 'hopeful undergraduates and medical students who became things of dark imaginings. . . . Whose passions had consumed themselves to dust'; who from their hero's poetry had deduced 'two great commandments, to hate your neighbour and to love your neighbour's wife'?

Quite simply Macaulay did not respond to Wordsworth's transcendentalism; he did respond to the Byronic mixture of man-of-the-world, violent passion and satire. For Macaulay, Byron excelled in description and meditation. 'The wonders of the outer world, the Tagus, with the mighty fleets of England riding on its bosom, the towers of Cintra overhanging the shaggy forest of cork-trees and willows, the glaring marble of Pentelicus, the banks of the Rhine, the glaciers of Clarens, the sweet Lake of Leman, the dell of Egeria with its summer-birds and rustling lizards, the shapeless ruins of Rome overgrown with ivy and wall-flowers, the stars, the sea, the mountains!' These were the 'accessories' to a single personage, whether called Harold or Lara or Manfred, 'proud, moody, cynical, with defiance on his brow, and misery in his heart, a scorner of his kind, implacable in revenge, yet capable of deep and strong affection'. There was of course also a woman, 'all softness and gentleness, loving to caress and to be caressed, but capable of being transformed by passion into a tigress!'. But in the end both were the poet: 'He was himself the beginning, the middle, and the end, of all his own poetry, the hero of every tale, the chief object in every landscape'.

Of this hero, Byron, Macaulay writes: 'From maniac laughter to piercing lamentation, there was not a single note of human anguish of which he was not master.' Miserable, satiated, withered in heart, defying the power of earth and heaven, scornful of society and at war with it—such was the *persona* Byron presented. 'That he was not such a person is beyond all doubt', Macaulay declares. Of course some of the morbidity may have been real, perhaps stemming 'from the nervousness of dissipation'. But, asks the realist Macaulay, would someone who so scorned his fellow-creatures publish three or four books a year to tell them so? Would he be so elated when his maiden speech in the Lords was praised? Sad he doubtless was, but 'the interest which his first confessions excited induced him to affect much that he did not feel; and the affectation probably reacted on his feelings'.

Time, Macaulay was sure, would sift Byron's poetry and much would be rejected as worthless; to another age he would be simply a writer not a personality. But, concludes Macaulay, 'after the closest scrutiny, there will still remain much that can only perish with the English language'. That, indeed, has happened. Macaulay, however, never explains why he is so sure it will.

An even better example of Macaulay's biographical-critical essays—and almost his last—came a dozen years later: his 'Life and Writings of Addison'. To Addison he felt bound by 'affection' though not, he hastens to add, by 'abject idolatry', and there were similarities; both were Whigs, both politicians and ministers as well as writers. They shared a middle-class, professional ancestry. They had 'got on'.

So naturally a certain idolatry comes through Macaulay's telling of the story of the shy, retiring Fellow of Magdalene who became the most influential man-of-letters in London, as well as Secretary of State and husband of the Dowager Countess of Warwick, 'unsullied statesman, master of pure English eloquence, consummate painter of life and manners, great satirist, who, without inflicting a wound, effected a great social reform'. Macaulay does not ignore Addison's short-comings; on the other hand, he never even hints that his conduct can be interpreted as sly, coldly self-seeking and pusillanimous. Nor today would most readers agree that Addison's contributions to the *Tatler, Spectator* and *Free-holder* show him either as a 'great satirist' or a 'consummate' guide to the life of his times. But he has certainly been greatly underestimated in the last forty or so years; and perhaps the greatest tribute to be paid to this essay is that it makes the reader's fingers itch to turn over the pages of Addison's contributions to the *Spectator* and even of his tragedy, *Cato*.

IV. POEMS

Of Macaulay's verse and particularly the *Lays of Ancient Rome* (1842), Saintsbury remarked that, though 'poetry for the million, nevertheless those who do not recognise the poetic quality in it show that their poetical thermometer is deficient in delicacy and range'. The *Lays*, enormously successful in the poet's day and long afterwards, sprang out of Macaulay's wide and deep classical reading fused, less obviously, with his love of English ballads, which he bought, almost compulsively, from the book-stalls, then a feature of many London streets. 'Every half-penny song on which he could lay his hands, he acquired', says Trevelyan, 'if only it was decent and a genuine, undoubted poem of the people'.

Macaulay believed, following Perizonius and supported by Niebuhr, that the tales of the birth of Romulus and Remus and the fight of the Horatii and the Curatii, related by Livy, sprang from ballads sung by the very early Romans, and long lost. He sought to re-create them using English ballad metre and was delighted to discover later that his 'Lars Porsena of Clusium', written in what he calls a catalectic dimeter iambic line, had a Latin source of sorts; at least an old grammarian recalled seeing 'Dabunt malum Metelli Naevio poetae', which resembled the beat of Macaulay's 'saturnian' line. The only parallel he could think of in English was in the nursery rhyme,

> The Queen was in her parlour
> Eating bread and honey.

The four *Lays* are supposed to be told by a minstrel living some three or four hundred years before Christ and himself recalling yet earlier legends. The narrator of 'Horatius' looks back about a hundred and twenty years and, says Macaulay in a preface, 'seems to have been an honest citizen, proud of the military glory of his country, sick of the disputes of factions, and much given to pining after good old times which never really existed'—all of which fitted Macaulay himself, despite his warning about nostalgia in the *History*. The *Lays* were intended to bring vividly to the mind's eye what he soberly calls 'some information about past times', which everyone 'not utterly savage longs for'. This aim differed not at all from the primal, private urge that drove Macaulay towards writing the *History*.

The *Lays* move fast, the story-line is clear, heroes and villains are immediately distinguishable, and an atmosphere of 'long ago' is breathed out imperceptibly as from a bowl of *pot-pourri*. The whole is pulled together, clinched, by the thumping rhythm and rhymes that are inevitable, not ingenious. 'The verses are not just easy to remember but almost impossible to forget', says one critic. The colours are primary, the drama as basic as in a child's dreams. Through all rings, triumphant, the trumpet note of high endeavour, 'backs against the wall' steadfastness, heroism against odds, the simple patriotism of an uncorrupted people in 'the brave days of old':

> Then out spake brave Horatius
> The Captain of the Gate:
> 'To every man upon this earth
> Death cometh soon or late.

And how can man die better
Than facing fearful odds,
For the ashes of his father
And the temples of his Gods'.

Macaulay treated of other historical subjects, as in 'Ivry: a song of the Huguenots'—

Now glory to the Lord of Hosts,
From whom all glories are!
And glory to our sovereign Liege,
King Henry of Navarre!

and made another sort of drama from an incident in Genesis ('The marriage of Tirzan and Ahirad'). He left only a fragment of 'The Armada' and the brief, echoing 'Epitaph on a Jacobite' who for his 'true King' threw away 'lands, honours, wealth, sway'—

And one dear hope, that was more prized than they.
For him I languished in a foreign clime,
Grey-haired with sorrow in my manhood's prime;
Heard on Lavernia Scargill's whispering trees,
And pined by Arno for my lovelier Tees . . .

Not surprisingly for one who had been at Trinity and in the Commons with Praed, Macaulay wrote *vers de societé* or *d'occasion*, often in letters to his sisters. Here he describes the magnificent dinner given by the banker Goldsmid to celebrate the Jewish emancipation Act:

I dined with a Jew,
Such Christians are few,
He gave me no ham,
But plenty of lamb,
And three sorts of fishes,
And thirty made dishes.
I drank his champagne
Again and again . . .
O Christians whose feasts
Are scarce fit for beasts,
Example take you—
By this worthy old Jew.

39

The only poem of deeper personal significance is that written the evening of his defeat in Edinburgh at the election of July, 1847. It is in the form of a dream of the 'fairy queens' attendant on his birth and of one last, mightiest and best—a 'glorious lady, with the eyes of light' who advises him to let go 'gain, fashion, pleasure, power': hers is 'the world of thought, the world of dream. Mine all the past, and all the future mine'. She, the Muse of History perhaps, tells him

> Yes; thou wilt love me with exceeding love;
> And I will tenfold all that love repay!

So, indeed, she did.

V. THE HISTORY

History was popular reading all over Western Europe in the 1830s and 1840s, and those who wrote it could become rich and famous. Apart from Gibbon and Hume, Voltaire and Niebuhr, Macaulay's friend Henry Hallam had a success with his *Constitutional History of England* in 1827, outdone only by Thomas Carlyle's *The French Revolution* ten years later.

Macaulay had long wished to join this happy band. He knew what he wanted to write about, namely English history from 1688 onwards, which even to educated people was, he thought, 'almost a terra incognita'; and he knew how he wanted to write it. It would be 'an amusing narrative . . . which shall for a few days supersede the last fashionable novel on the tables of young ladies'. He later corrected this: 'I have had the year 2000 and even the year 3000 often in my mind.'

He would reclaim from such novelists as Scott and Sismondi that part of the historian's role they had appropriated. The historian, too, should seek 'to make the past present, to bring the distant near, to place us in the society of a great man or on the eminence which overlooks the field of a mighty battle . . . to call up our ancestors before us with all their peculiarities of language, manners and garb, to show us over their houses, to seat us at their tables, to rummage their old-fashioned wardrobes, to explain the uses of their ponderous furniture.'

He, too, should lay 'before us all the springs of motion and all the causes of decay . . . tracing the connection of causes and effects . . . we should not have to look for the wars and votes of the Puritans in Clarendon, and for their phraseology in *Old Mortality;* for one half of King James in Hume, and for the other half in *The Fortunes of Nigel.*'

Of course the historian must relate no fact, attribute no expression to his characters which is not authenticated by sufficient testimony. In any case, he loved facts and '*minute* touches'. He felt that almost metaphysical sense of the past and urgent need to share in the thoughts and feelings of men long dead, to handle the very document Cromwell indited, to tread, as Keats wrote, 'the heath where Druids old have been, where mantles grey have rustled by . . .'. Gibbon, striding the ruins of the Forum and standing on the spot 'where Romulus stood, or Tully spoke, or Caesar fell,' described it as 'intoxication'.

Macaulay prepared himself well. He ransacked French and Dutch archives. He turned over thousands of pamphlets and ballads collected from frowsty shops and street stalls. He worked in libraries at Lambeth, the British Museum and Edinburgh. At All Souls', he discovered in Narcissus Luttrell's diary such *curiosa* as that the Jacobites drank treasonable healths by limping round the room with glasses at their lips ('To limp meant L. Louis XIV, I. James, M., Mary of Modena, P. Prince of Wales'). The Tanner, Wharton, Nairne MSS were devoured. He tramped Londonderry with old maps; he saw Glencoe ('the very valley of the shadow of death') and Killiecrankie; and he knew York, Bristol and Norwich as well as he knew London.

Down it all went into a multitude of notebooks. Printed accounts he accumulated in his own library; and behind him he had a lifetime of almost incontinent reading—from Homer and Thucydides ('The Great Historian') to Bacon, Burke ('the greatest Englishman since Milton'), Voltaire, von Ranke, Southey, Niebuhr. Underpinning all was a phenomenal photographic memory.

When he had the details of an episode clear in his head, the inconsistencies in sources sorted out, and the 'humour' was upon him, 'he would sit down and write off the whole story at a headlong pace . . . securing in black and white each idea, and epithet, and turn of phrase, as it flowed straight from his busy brain to his rapid fingers. His manuscript, at this stage, to the eyes of anyone but himself, appeared to consist of column after column of dashes and flourishes, in which a straight line, with a half-formed letter at each end, and another in the middle, did duty for a word'.

From this rough draft he would next morning write out in a large hand and with many erasures a full version, seldom doing more than six pages a day because, says Trevelyan, he knew by experience that 'this was as much as he could do at his best; and except when he was at his best, he never would work at all'. When the thoughts and words ceased to flow fast, he stopped writing. He never, however, stopped revising. Often he rewrote a chapter for the sake of 'a more lucid arrangement'. Every word was scrutinized and, if he thought it appropriate, none was rejected because it was unknown to Swift and Dryden. So, we find such contemporary-sounding nouns as 'squatters', secrets being 'blabbed', buildings being 'gutted' (a 'coarse metaphor', he admits) and military duties being 'shirked'—a word, he says, used by high and low because it is the 'only word for the thing'. In his Journal he was matter-of-fact about his 'impotency and despondency' when he found 'arrangement and transition' difficult, and frank about 'sewing on a grand purple patch'.

All that he intended he achieved, except that his *History of England from the Accession of James II* scarcely reached the death of William III in 1702, some one hundred and fifty years short of the target, and even this event takes place in a fragmentary and posthumous Vol. V, put together by his sister. The *History* as it stands is incomplete and inevitably out of balance. Macaulay covers the first 2,000 or so years of British (rather than English) history, from the discovery of the inhabitants by 'the Tyrian mariners, the Phoenicians', to the restoration of Charles II, in a mere 160 pages. The subsequent 1200 or so pages are given to forty-two years, of which two reigns of some seventeen years take up the bulk of the space. He had sacrificed his grand harmonious design, lengthening his history by shortening its time span.

The unity of the work is best conveyed in the first two volumes. The forward rush gets under way as Monk and his Scottish army march into England and declare a free parliament. 'The bells of all England rang joyously: the gutters ran with ale; and night after night, the sky five miles round London was reddened by innumerable bonfires'. Charles lands at Dover whose cliffs are 'covered by thousands of gazers' and, despite the coolness of the troops drawn up on Blackheath, the 'restored wanderer', is soon reposing 'safe in the palace of his ancestors.' Then comes a quieter passage, picking up momentum again as the Cavaliers become violent, Clarendon falls, Danby falls, the Papists plot, Louis plots and the conflict between the Crown and Parliament seems about to be brought 'to a final issue'.

Next comes a halt of 120 pages, during which he makes social history respectable; then the pounding course resumes, interspersed with quieter moods, the death-bed of Charles II, the sly and slimy hugger-mugger of spies, until with crashing and discordant chords we come to the execution of Monmouth ('It was ten o'clock. The coach of the lieutenant of the Tower was made ready . . .'), and the vengeance of Jeffreys in the West, the Bloody Assizes and executions everywhere: 'a time of misery, and terror', and as the blood and fury ebb, the dissenting spirit is left cowed. There is only the 'good' Bishop Ken to soften the harsh, cruel notes. Then, as the dire autumn of 1685 crawls to its end, come intimations of Spring and 'the first faint indications of a great turn of fortune'.

Hopefully we take up Volume II, only to discover that Spring is delayed. Still twisted and twisting, James II is at 'the height of power and prosperity', his enemies' courage 'effectually quelled'. We are vouchsafed a temporary glimpse of hope—William of Orange, married to James's daughter Mary. But that glimpse swiftly fades; not for many a long dissonant page of miseries and faithlessness do we see him again, now setting sail for England. Optimism grows as gradually as William's advance—almost a saunter, with stumbles—from his landing at Torbay through the West Country to Hungerford, while James makes frantic

43

attempts to get his Queen and the Prince of Wales out of the country.

Then, a grand climax: the Prince and Princess of Orange stand beneath the canopy of state in Inigo Jones' magnificent Banqueting House in Whitehall. Lords and Commons move towards them, bow low; William and Mary step a few paces forward, the Declaration of Right is read in a loud voice, William and Mary accept the Crown. A sudden piercing 'shout of joy is heard in the streets below, and is instantly answered by huzzas from many thousands of voices. . . . The heralds and poursuivants were waiting in their gorgeous tabards. All the space as far as Charing Cross was one sea of heads. The kettle drums struck up; the trumpets pealed . . .'

The volume closes calmly, 'all passion spent', with Macaulay musing over the peacefulness of the Revolution, 'conducted with strict attention to ancient formalities'. With some complacence he contrasts it with the revolutions raging, as he writes in 1848, in the proudest capitals of Western Europe now streaming with 'civil blood . . . evil passions . . . the antipathy of class to class, race to race. . . .' And so to the final, firm chord: 'For the authority of law, for the security of property, for the peace of our streets, for the happiness of our homes, our gratitude is due under him who raises and pulls down nations at his pleasure, to the Long Parliament, to the Convention and to William of Orange'.

Volumes III and IV, which appeared in 1855, some seven years after the first two volumes, are different. The drive towards a glorious consummation is gone. The focus is steadily on William, to whom all the threads of the story lead. Events occur and are dramatically described: the battle of the Boyne, Glencoe, Steinkirk, Landen. The recoinage is remarked and the quarrel about Darien, but all are linked with William. These two volumes and the posthumous one are largely a biography of the King.

Nevertheless, wherever in the whole *History* the reader dips, he is likely to go on reading page after page. This is a testimony to Macaulay's art. He knows how to alternate long and short sentences in consonance with what he is describing. Wherever possible he uses dialogue, and where appropriate devices from rhetoric such as anaphora and antitheses, usually to sum up: 'The liberality of the nation had been made fruitless by the vices of the government'. He sometimes uses the dramatist's trick of raising tension by delaying a *dénouement*.

His devices are seldom employed merely to dazzle. The paradox that 'we owe more to the weaknesses and mean-nesses (of James I) than to the wisdom and courage of much better sovereigns' is true. The striking phrase is everywhere: Charles I's great qualities were spoiled by 'an incurable pro-pensity to dark and crooked ways', even though his execution was 'not only a crime but an error'. We really see that London mob 'hopping and crawling in crowds', and William 'carried away in fits from Mary's dying bed'. Bishop Burnet is 'a living dictionary of British affairs'. Macaulay is adept, too, at tossing in ideas that may still provoke thought: 'It is better that men should be governed by priestcraft than by brute force'; or, at the close of the reign of Charles II, there was 'not a single English painter or statuary whose name is now re-membered'. And speaking of his own time he says 'the pro-gress of civilization has diminished the physical comforts of a portion of the poorest class'.

The *History* is also a gallery of portraits, done in primary colours and with the broad strokes of a Pre-Raphaelite. Their literary provenance includes the seventeenth century 'charac-ter', harking back to Theophrastus, made popular by Hall, Sir Thomas Overbury, Earle's *Microcosmography*. Sometimes, but not always, Macaulay draws a character as either Simon Pure or as the devil lacking only the horns.

His Judge Jeffreys, who is heralded as that 'wicked judge' whose 'depravity' has become proverbial, is unrelievedly horrid. As he condemns men, 'their weeping and imploring seemed to titillate him voluptuously'. He sends a woman to be scourged at the cart's tail with the instruction to the hang-man: 'Scourge her till the blood runs down! It is Christmas, a cold day for madam to strip in! See that you warm her shoulders thoroughly!' Jeffreys himself is a drunkard and we are shown him stripped naked with an equally drunken Lord Treasurer attempting to climb a signpost to drink the King's health; he is also a turncoat. He exacts an appalling ven-geance throughout the West Country after Monmouth's rebellion, leaving behind him carnage, mourning and terror. He is cordially welcomed back from his campaign in the West by a delighted James II, who recounts with glee to the aghast foreign ambassadors the horrors Jeffreys had committed. The picture of Jeffreys, as we now know from the researches of G. W. Keeton, is flawed by great exaggeration and as great omissions.[1]

Macaulay leaves James II with scarcely a shred of reputation. Yet Charles II, whom politically and morally he condemned, is done in curiously soft colours. He acts (over the Exclusion Bill) from 'a sense of duty, and honour'. Careless and profuse as he was with money for his pleasures, he does spare a sum to form a 'little army' which was the germ of 'that great and renowned army which has, in the present century, marched triumphant into Madrid and Paris, into Canton and Candahar'. Though Charles's temper could be harsh, he had an easy way of allowing 'all persons who had been properly introduced' to 'see him dine, sup, dance and play at hazard'—the lion allowing the public to watch him feed—and hear him tell the stories, which indeed he told remarkably well, of his flight from Worcester and the miseries he endured as state prisoner 'at the hands of the canting, meddling preachers of Scotland'. These sociable habits, Macaulay declares, proved 'a far more successful Kingcraft than any that his father or grandfather had practised'.

Of course, Charles was a liar, he had more than dubious dealings with the French, he thought that every person was to be bought, that integrity was a trick by which 'clever men kept up the price of their abilities', that the love of God, country, family, friends were synonyms for the love of self. All the same Macaulay had a soft spot for him and devoted every skill he possessed to describe at length the comings-and-goings around Charles's death bed. After the illness first shows itself, we see him 'chatting and toying with three women, whose charms were the boast and whose vices were the 'disgrace, of three nations', while 'some amorous verses were warbled'. Then he collapses, face black, eyes turning

[1]*Lord Chancellor Jeffreys and the Stuart cause*, by G. W. Keeton (Macdonald, 1965).

in his head; the Duchess of Portsmouth hangs over him 'with the familiarity of a wife' in an 'agony of grief'; she is forced to retire by the arrival of the Queen, who is so affected that she faints and is 'carried senseless to her chamber'.

Now the Anglican prelates besiege him, fruitlessly, but the Duchess, despite her 'life of frivolity and vice', retained 'all that kindness which is the glory of her sex', and knew that the King in his few serious moments was a Roman Catholic. She sends to find a priest, and in great secrecy, through a back door, an illiterate Benedictine is brought in—a cloak over his sacred vestments, 'his shaven crown concealed by a flowing wig'. He gives the King communion, but he cannot swallow the bread until water is brought. Next day, after apologising for being an unconscionable time dying, he died: 'the last glimpse', wrote Macaulay, 'of that exquisite urbanity, so often found potent to charm away the resentment of a justly incensed patron'.

The reader has the strong impression that he is watching events as they happen. The illusion is created also in the description of Monmouth's trial and death, and of the battle of the Boyne. People seem to move before our eyes: Seymour, 'looking like what he is, the chief of a dissolute and high-spirited gentry, with the artificial ringlets clustering in fashionable profusion round his shoulders, and a mingled expression of voluptuousness and disdain in his eye and on his lip'; Titus Oates, 'legs uneven, the vulgar said, as those of a badger, his forehead low as that of a baboon, his purple cheeks, his monstrous length of chin'. Macaulay can create his effect even with groups of people, such as the extreme Puritan known by his gait, his lank hair, the sour solemnity of his face, the upturned whites of his eyes, his nasal twang and his peculiar dialect.

He used his gift for personalizing groups of people and bringing dull facts to life with notable power in his celebrated 'sociological' chapter iii, Vol. I, in which he describes the general state of the country when James II came to the throne. The country was physically different from the one the Victorians knew. In 1685, the wilder parts—Cumberland and Northumberland—were unmapped, the paths a local secret, the forests larger and impenetrable, tenanted by wolves, wild bulls with white manes, wailing wild cats and troops of huge bustards.

The roads were such that Pepys and his wife in their coach lost their way between Newbury and Reading. To travel by public coach Macaulay discovers, cost 2½d. a mile in summer and rather more in winter. He casts his eyes down and sees that the floors of dining rooms were 'coloured brown with a wash made of soot and small beer, to hide the dirt'. In those days, too, St. James's Square was the receptacle of offal, cinders, and all the dead dogs of Westminster under the very windows 'of the gilded saloons in which the first magnates of the realm, Norfolks, Ormonds, Kents and Pembrokes, gave banquets and balls'. He examines the immense variety of coffee-houses—the Londoner's home—and finds that some were frequented by Puritans: Jews, 'dark-eyed money changers from Venice and Amsterdam', also had their own special places.

He notes that the average wage for the labouring classes was four shillings a week in agriculture, while those who tended looms received one shilling a day, and a bricklayer 2s. 6d. The well-paid Macaulay observes with dismay that the famous Dryden's *Fables* brought him only £250 for the copyright—'less than in our days has sometimes been paid for two articles in a review'. Nor does he overlook 'the seats of industry', Manchester ('a busy and opulent place', but without a single coach), Sheffield's forges and Birmingham's buttons.

Then skilfully varying his approach, Macaulay focuses on a person, a type, and breathes life into him. The young chaplain attached to the household of 'the coarse and ignorant squire ... cast up the farrier's bill. He walked ten miles with a message or a parcel. ... He might fill himself with the corned beef and carrots; but, as soon as the tarts and cheesecakes made their appearance, he quitted his seat and stood aloof till he was summoned to return thanks for the repast, from a great part of which he had been excluded. ... A waiting woman was generally considered as the most suitable help-mate for a parson ... the chaplain was the resource of a lady's maid whose reputation had been blown upon'.

Macaulay was always immensely interested in inventions

and industrial processes, so he praises the 'Royal Society for the improvement of natural knowledge', founded in 1660. Although its new philosophy bred 'dreams of wings with which men were to fly from the Tower to the Abbey', Macaulay recognizes that its pottering with hydrostatics, barometers, airpumps, telescopes and a microscope which 'made a fly look as large as a sparrow', were the beginning of a 'long series of glorious and salutary reforms. . . . Already a reform of agriculture had been commenced . . . medicine became an experimental and progressive science. . . . One after another phantoms which had haunted the world through ages of darkness fled before the light. Astrology and alchemy became jests. . . .' Wallis, Haley, Flamsteed and of course the great Isaac Newton are singled out as the heirs of the spirit of Francis Bacon experimenting with refrigeration in the snow, a spirit 'compounded of audacity and sobriety'.

What the whole *History* exhales, like an unknown perfume, is the strangeness of our seventeenth century ancestors. They seem, in Macaulay's pages, to be as foreign as Trobrian islanders, their emotions volatile as a baby's, their tolerance of horrors enormously high. The Whigs, Macaulay tells us, murmured because Stafford was allowed to die 'without seeing his bowels burned before his face'. It seemed proper that the wicked should be drawn and quartered while yet alive. At the same time, the arts of the age were often exquisite, full of sentiment and suffused with pathos. Their attitude to death, including their own, was often casual. They lived with a sense of eternity stretching before them, so what mattered was not their departure to it, but whether they died in a faith guaranteeing them heaven rather than hell. Hence the overwhelming importance of religious differences.

It is hard to disagree with Macaulay's belief that the national character has been mollified, that people had become 'kinder' and more humane. We now have, he writes, a 'sensitive and restless compassion . . . which winces at every lash laid on the back of a drunken soldier' and extends 'a powerful protection to the factory child, to the Hindoo widow, to the negro slave'. Life had become longer, health better, communications faster.

This process Macaulay sometimes refers to as 'betterment'

49

or 'improvement', which can scarcely be denied, and some-times as 'progress' which has always been disputed. 'Progress to what and from where?' inquired Disraeli. 'The European talks of progress because by an ingenious application of some scientific acquirements he has established a society which has mistaken comfort for civilization'. Or, put another way, it is mistaken to equate progress with happiness.

While from Macaulay's vantage point in history it might seem that men had become more humane and would con-tinue further along that way, he had no smallest prevision of the murderous world wars, the institution of state slavery enforced by torture and murder in the totalitarian states of Europe, the 'liberation' of India and Africa to killing and rapine. To us, Macaulay's sentence that 'no man who is correctly informed as to the past will be disposed to take a morose or desponding view of the present' has a sour ring.

VI. THE HISTORY UNDER FIRE

Reading the *History* is a tremendous experience but, as Macaulay himself confessed, there are in it 'real blemishes as I too well know!'

Some details of the period he did not and could not be aware of, because the documents were not then available; for example the letters from King William to his friend the Prince of Waldeck, or the conversations recorded between the King and Halifax. Sometimes he simply ignored matters important to his text, such as the 'Settlement' Act of 1662 which prevented labourers moving from one parish to another in search of work, or overlooked whole areas of history such as the growth of England's trade with America and other colonies, now recognized as being the most re-markable development in economic history in the latter half of the seventeenth century. While the *loss* of the American colonies interested him greatly (see his essay on Chatham), their acquisition went unnoted, and the only colonies to which he devotes attention are India and Ireland. A little Englander indeed.

His account of William's landing in England is partly vitiated by his omitting the numbers in the opposing forces, so rendering the military situation unintelligible. Sufficiently precise figures were given in the sources he used. Sometimes he leaves out material facts, occasionally using the least trustworthy sources, with no worthier motive than to make a better story.

For James II he had twice the number of sources available to his predecessor Hume. He tries to evaluate them, but not systematically or with the critical, minute analysis that his near contemporary, Ranke practised. Nor does he always cite his sources with care: quoting from Evelyn's diary he gives the date of the entry, quoting from Luttrell's 'Brief Historical Relation' he does not. Airily, he directs us to Harrington's vast *Oceana*, without indicating the exact locus; blandly he refers to one of his sources as 'nauseous balderdash, but I have been forced to descend even lower, if possible, in search of materials'. A spate of close, accurate annotation of Barillon and Burnet is followed by an apparently dogmatic claim without reference to any authority at all.

He could be very stubborn in his inaccuracy. He was totally wrong about William Penn, even to confusing him with an unrelated George Penn. When this was pointed out in time for a second edition, he refused to correct: he had formed his conception of Penn early on and was adamant in conserving it, even haranguing into silence a group of Quakers who visited him to protest. Did he pass too lightly over continental politics? 'I am writing a History of *England*' was his haughty reply.

His figures for executions and transportations at the 'Bloody' Assizes are exaggerated. He says 300 were executed; the real figure was less than 150. He pictures Jeffreys as a devil from whom only the horns, the fork and the tail are missing. He does so by extracting spicy items from gossipy pamphlets of doubtful veracity, such as those of John Tutchin, himself sent to prison by Jeffreys. He even puts words into Jeffreys's mouth. The punishments imposed he suggests were Jeffreys's inventions, such as whipping at the cart-tail; in fact, they were still lawful in Macaulay's early years. He overlooks the fact that the strict rules governing the admissibility of evidence had not then been promulgated, and that the law's refusal to allow legal representation in cases of treason and felony positively compelled judges to take an active part in examining witnesses.

Then there was Marlborough who, Macaulay tells us, 'to those who can look steadily through the dazzling blaze of genius and glory' is really 'a prodigy of turpitude'. This is a distortion. That Marlborough was not always high-minded and was capable of deceit, that he entered into treasonable communication with James II, that he had a sexual liaison with the Duchess of Cleveland, are true, but he was something else as well, (as Macaulay elsewhere recognized). In the *History* he was cast in the role of villain and nothing should turn aside the shower of barbs Macaulay designed for him: 'insatiable of riches . . . at twenty he made money of his beauty and vigour; at sixty he made money of his genius and glory', 'thrifty in his very vices', master of a 'hundred villainies'. C. H. Firth believed that Macaulay's refusal to see the nobler side of Marlborough—which of course he might have shown in the unwritten volumes of the *History*—was due to his suspicion that Marlborough plotted to overthrow King William, put Anne in his place and so become himself Director of the civil and military government. No evidence for such a plot exists.

A more general criticism is that Macaulay's characters rarely change and grow, that they are composed of antitheses simulating the complexity of human beings, rather than drawn from observation. Or as Lord Morley put it 'he did not find his way to the indwelling man of many of his figures'. Macaulay describes, no one better, 'the *spectacle* of a character', wrote Walter Bagehot; of the depths of the psyche there is no hint. Nor, as W. J. Dawson wrote, does he show any sense of the mystery of living, whence we came and why we all, heroes and villains alike, tread the road to death. The eternal silence of these infinite spaces terrified Pascal; Macaulay had never noticed them. Life to him was a brilliant pageant; it did not occur to him that 'we are such stuff as dreams are made on'.

Even the tumultuous onward drive of the *History*, enjoyed by most readers, was objected to by Carlyle who said Macaulay 'is all very well for a time, but one wouldn't live under Niagara'. Again, Macaulay knew from the inside how politics worked: he was one of the many Victorian historians— Grote, Acton, Lecky, Bryce—who were in parliament and public life. Yet Morley, an M.P. and ex-Minister, wrote that the way Macaulay described the workings of politics was not the 'way in which things happen'.

It was, however, Cotter Morison in 1882 who first fired the big gun, whose trigger subsequently became worn with pressing, against Macaulay, the charge being that as a Whig he interpreted all his history from a party point of view. Macaulay, according to Morison, compared all past history 'to its disparagement with the present . . . to show how vastly the period of which he treats has been outstripped by the period in which he lives . . . a matter utterly indifferent to scientific history'. In short, Macaulay was biased.

Macaulay was not, of course, a Whig historian in the sense that Dr Johnson, a Tory, said of his early parliamentary reporting, 'I always saw to it that the Whig dogs had the worst of it'. Often in Macaulay the Tory dogs, such as Bishop Ken or Jeremy Collier, had the best of it, and he wrote in Volume I, chapter I of the *History* that 'the truth is that, though both parties have often seriously erred, England could have spared neither. . . . The two great sections of English politicians has always been a difference rather of degree than of principle'. All the same, he extenuates in William what he deplores in James and is more aware of moral defects in a Tory than in a Whig. He is certain that the Whigs wrested the Crown's prerogatives for the people, destroyed the Star Chamber, carried the Habeas Corpus Act, effected the glorious Revolution of 1688: in short to them we owe it that we have a House of Commons.

That Macaulay's Whig interpretation of history was no more than one possible interpretation was demonstrated by Professor Herbert Butterfield in 1931. Professor C. H. Firth in his *Commentary on Macaulay's History* (1936) offered a Tory reply: the vaunted Whig 'progress' was not always in the right direction; the Whigs by attempting in 1640 to overthrow the existing government of the Church of England and to substitute a Presbyterian system, caused the first Civil

War, and by their aggressive intolerance to all who were not Presbyterians caused the second Civil War in 1648. The Whigs' intolerance made a settlement in Ireland impossible; their fanatical hatred of Catholicism and their attempt to place a pretender on the English throne caused the futile struggle over the Exclusion bills and the yet more futile Monmouth rebellion, and so on.

Today, it is all *vieux jeu*. Popular history is propagandist to a degree Macaulay never dreamed of, and Voltaire's cynical view prevails, that history is 'a pack of tricks we play on the dead'. Serious history on the other hand, has become a matter of econometrics and the computer. Macaulay's 'the people thought' and 'a majority favoured' are replaced by detailed answers as to 'how many people' and 'what actual percentage'. The change is helpful, but it does not obviate our need for a historian who can tell a tale which holdeth children from play and old men from the chimney corner.

The need is increasingly recognized. A leading living historian, A. J. P. Taylor, condemning as unforgivable in a historian 'tired metaphors and flabby sentences', boldly asserts that, 'Although history may claim to be a branch of science or of politics or of sociology, it is primarily communication, a form of literature. No historian is worth his salt who has not felt some twinge of Macaulay's ambition— to replace the latest novel on the lady's dressing table. It is to the credit of English history at the present time that some historians have felt this ambition and a few have even accomplished it'—not least, of course, Taylor himself.

Even Macaulay's concentration on politics and government as the central core of history, so often derided in the socio-economic 1930s, is upheld by such as Sir George Clark on the grounds that 'It is in public institutions that men express their will to control events', and by others because government is the 'synthesising element' from which flow most other things, even the 'cultural qualities of an age'. Macaulay's idea of progress, to which two world wars seemed adequate refutation, is now defended. Dr. J. H. Plumb sees the idea as providing historians with an escape from stultifying fact-grubbing and myth-destruction. We *have* progressed: this is a 'great human truth, and if we accept it and explore its consequences history would not only be an infinitely richer education but also play a much, more effective part in the culture of Western society.'

So the critical winds seem to be blowing in Macaulay's favour again. Undoubtedly the *History* is still the best introduction to the brief period it covers; and most of the errors and *lacunae* could be put right by means of thorough annotation.[1] The book is worth it. As Lord Acton told Mary Gladstone, 'Read him, therefore, to find out how it comes that the most unsympathetic of critics (i.e. Acton) can think him very nearly the greatest of English writers.'

[1]There was such an annotation by T. F. Henderson, but published as long ago as 1907 and so not including much later material.

MACAULAY

A Select Bibliography

(Place of publication London, unless stated otherwise)

Collected Works:

THE WORKS, ed. Lady Trevelyan, 8 vols (1866).
THE WORKS, 12 vols (1898)
—the Albany Edition.
THE WORKS, 9 vols [1906–07]
—Vols IV–VIII, *The History of England*, edited by T. F. Henderson.

Selected Works:

SELECTIONS FROM THE ESSAYS AND SPEECHES, 2 vols (1856).
SELECTIONS FROM THE WRITINGS, ed. G. O. Trevelyan (1876).
SELECTIONS, ed. E. V. Downs and G. L. Davis (1930).
THE READERS' MACAULAY: A Selection from His Essays, Letters and History of England, ed. W. H. French and G. D. Sanders; New York (1936).
LORD MACAULAY'S LEGISLATIVE MINUTES, sel. C. D. Dharker; Madras (1946).
MACAULAY: PROSE AND POETRY, ed. G. M. Young (1953).

Separate Works:

POMPEII; Cambridge (1819)
—awarded the Chancellor's Medal for English verse, 1819.
EVENING; Cambridge (1821)
—awarded the Chancellor's Medal for English verse, 1821.
LAYS OF ANCIENT ROME (1842)
—the edition of 1848 included also 'Ivry' and 'The Armada'. Edited by G. M. Trevelyan in the World's Classics, 1928.
CRITICAL AND HISTORICAL ESSAYS CONTRIBUTED TO THE EDINBURGH REVIEW, 3 vols (1843)
—frequently reprinted. The standard edition edited by F. C. Montague, 3 vols, 1903; Everyman's Library, 2 vols, 1907; Oxford Edition, 2 vols, 1913.
THE HISTORY OF ENGLAND FROM THE ACCESSION OF JAMES II, 5 vols (1849–61)
—in 8 vols, with a Memoir by H. H. Milman, 1858–62; Everyman's Library, 3 vols, 1906; illustrated edition by C. H. Firth, 6 vols, 1913–15; World's Classics, edited by T. F. Henderson, 5 vols, 1931.
SPEECHES, PARLIAMENTARY AND MISCELLANEOUS, 2 vols (1854).

SPEECHES, ed. G. M. Young (1935)
—in the World's Classics.

THE INDIAN CIVIL SERVICE: Report to the Rt Hon. Sir C. Wood, Bart, by T. B. Macaulay, Lord Ashburton, The Revd. H. Melvill, B. Jowett and the Speaker of the House of Commons (1855).

THE MISCELLANEOUS WRITINGS, ed. T. F. Ellis. 2 vols (1860)
—best reprint, Everyman's Library, 2 vols, 1910. Contains his contributions, essays and poems to *Knight's Quarterly Magazine* (1823–24) and the five biographies he wrote for the English edition of the *Encyclopaedia Britannica* (1854–59).

THE INDIAN EDUCATION MINUTES now first collected from records in the Department of Public Instructions. Edited by G. Woodrow, Calcutta (1862).

THE LETTERS OF MACAULAY, vols I–III, edited by J. Pinney (1974–76)
—Professor Pinney's long introduction and notes are very valuable.

Some Critical and Biographical Studies:

MR MACAULAY'S CHARACTER OF THE CLERGY IN THE LATTER PART OF THE SEVENTEENTH CENTURY CONSIDERED, by C. Babington; Cambridge (1849).

WILLIAM PENN: An historical biography by W. H. Dixon (1851)
—doubts Macaulay's portrait of Penn with apparent justification.

AN INQUIRY INTO THE EVIDENCE RELATING TO THE CHARGES BROUGHT BY LORD MACAULAY AGAINST WILLIAM PENN, by J. Paget; Edinburgh (1858).

THE NEW 'EXAMEN', OR AN INQUIRY INTO THE EVIDENCE RELATING TO CERTAIN PASSAGES IN LORD MACAULAY'S HISTORY, by J. Paget; Edinburgh & London (1861)
—reprinted, with an introduction by Winston Churchill, 1934.

THE PUBLIC LIFE OF LORD MACAULAY, by F. Arnold (1862).

A MEMOIR OF LORD MACAULAY, by H. H. Milman (1862).

JERROLD, TENNYSON AND MACAULAY, by J. H. Stirling; Edinburgh (1868).

BIOGRAPHICAL SKETCHES, by H. Martineau (1869).

CRITICAL MISCELLANIES, by J. Morley, vol II, (1871–77).

THE LIFE AND LETTERS, ed. G. O. Trevelyan, 2 vols, O.U.P. (1876)
—by Macaulay's nephew and still the best complete biography also containing extracts from the journals, World Classics edition, 2 vols (1932).

INDEX TO TREVELYAN'S LIFE AND LETTERS OF LORD MACAULAY, by Perceval Clark (1907)
—Longmans for the Index Society.

HOURS IN A LIBRARY, by L. Stephen. Series III (1874–79).

GLEANINGS OF PAST YEARS, 1843–78, by W. E. Gladstone, 7 vols (1879).

LITERARY STUDIES, by W. Bagehot, ed. R. H. Hutton, 2 vols (1879).
 Everyman's Library edition, edited by G. Sampson (1911).

LORD MACAULAY, ESSAYIST AND HISTORIAN, by A. S. G. Canning (1882)
—revised and extended edition (1913).

MACAULAY, by J. C. Morison (1882)
—in the 'English Men of Letters' series.

STUDIES IN EARLY VICTORIAN LITERATURE, by F. Harrison (1895)
—contains 'Macaulay's Place in Literature'.

MACAULAY: A Lecture, by R. C. Jebb; Cambridge (1900).

STRAY PAPERS, by W. M. Thackeray (1901)
—contains 'Mr Macaulay's Essays'.

THE MAKERS OF MODERN PROSE, by W. J. Dawson (1899)
—two chapters on Macaulay, giving the general critical attitude to him
 at the turn of the century.

ESSAYS AND ADDRESSES, 1900–1903, by Lord Avebury (1903).

THE MARGINAL NOTES OF LORD MACAULAY, selected and arranged by
 G. O. Trevelyan (1907).

CLIO: A MUSE, by G. M. Trevelyan (1913).

LORD MACAULAY: The Pre-Eminent Victorian, by S. C. Roberts (1927)
—English Association pamphlet, No 67. Reprinted in *An Eighteenth-
 Century Gentleman and Other Essays* (1930).

CHAPTERS OF AUTOBIOGRAPHY, by A. J. Balfour (1930).

MACAULAY, by A. Bryant (1932).

A COMMENTARY ON MACAULAY'S HISTORY OF ENGLAND, by C. H. Firth
 (1938)
—very fair consideration of the criticisms of Macaulay's historical
 accuracy, voiced before his death and subsequently by J. Paget.
 Firth's lectures were given before 1914 so he was unable to consider
 criticisms made by Winston Churchill in *Marlborough, his Life and
 Times* (1933–34).

THE ENGLISH UTILITARIANS AND INDIA, by E. Stokes; Oxford (1959).

MACAULAY, by M. A. Thomson (1959)
—published in the Historical Association's general series, No. 42.

MACAULAY'S LIBRARY, by A. N. L. Munby; Glasgow (1966)
—David Murray Foundation Lecture, University of Glasgow, 9 March,
 1965.

LORD MACAULAY 1800–1859, by D. Knowles; Cambridge (1960).

THE NATURE OF HISTORY, by A. Marwick (1970)
—useful references to Macaulay in a historiographical context.

THOMAS BABINGTON MACAULAY. The Shaping of the Historian, by J.
 Clive (1973)
—excellent study but ends before the *History* was begun.

MACAULAY, by J. Millgate (1973)
—in Routledge's Author's Guide series—the best bibliography.
STYLE IN HISTORY, by P. Gay (1975)
—contains a stimulating essay on 'Macaulay, Intellectual Voluptuary'.

Note: The Macaulay MSS of diaries from which Trevelyan quoted selectively are in the library of Trinity College, Cambridge. The British Library has collections of MSS about Macaulay's friends such as Macvey Nagies, Lord and Lady Holland, etc. Macaulay family material is at the Huntington Library in California, London University Library has smaller collections of such material.

WRITERS AND THEIR WORK

SMOLLETT: Laurence Brander
STEELE, ADDISON: A. R. Humphreys
STERNE: D. W. Jefferson
SWIFT: J. Middleton Murry (1955)
SWIFT: A. Norman Jeffares (1976)
VANBRUGH: Bernard Harris
HORACE WALPOLE: Hugh Honour

Nineteenth Century:
ARNOLD: Kenneth Allott
AUSTEN: S. Townsend Warner (1951)
AUSTEN: B. C. Southam (1975)
BAGEHOT: N. St John-Stevas
THE BRONTË SISTERS:
          Phyllis Bentley (1950)
THE BRONTËS: I & II: Winifred Gérin
E. B. BROWNING: Alethea Hayter
ROBERT BROWNING: John Bryson
SAMUEL BUTLER: G. D. H. Cole
BYRON: I, II & III: Bernard Blackstone
CARLYLE: David Gascoyne
CARROLL: Derek Hudson
CLOUGH: Isobel Armstrong
COLERIDGE: Kathleen Raine
CREEVEY & GREVILLE: J. Richardson
DE QUINCEY: Hugh Sykes Davies
DICKENS: K. J. Fielding
    EARLY NOVELS: T. Blount
    LATER NOVELS: B. Hardy
DISRAELI: Paul Bloomfield
GEORGE ELIOT: Lettice Cooper
FITZGERALD: Joanna Richardson
GASKELL: Miriam Allott
GISSING: A. C. Ward
HARDY: R. A. Scott-James
          and C. Day Lewis
HAZLITT: J. B. Priestley
HOOD: Laurence Brander
HOPKINS: Geoffrey Grigson
T. H. HUXLEY: William Irvine
KEATS: Edmund Blunden (1950)
KEATS: Miriam Allott (1976)
LAMB: Edmund Blunden
LANDOR: G. Rostrevor Hamilton
LEAR: Joanna Richardson
MACAULAY: G. R. Potter (1959)
MACAULAY: Kenneth Young (1976)
MEREDITH: Phyllis Bartlett

MILL: Maurice Cranston
MORRIS: P. Henderson
NEWMAN: J. M. Cameron
PATER: Ian Fletcher
PEACOCK: J. I. M. Stewart
CHRISTINA ROSSETTI: G. Battiscombe
D. G. ROSSETTI: Oswald Doughty
RUSKIN: Peter Quennell
SCOTT: Ian Jack
SHELLEY: G. M. Matthews
SOUTHEY: Geoffrey Carnall
STEPHEN: Phyllis Grosskurth
STEVENSON: G. B. Stern
SWINBURNE: Ian Fletcher
TENNYSON: B. C. Southam
THACKERAY: Laurence Brander
FRANCIS THOMPSON: P. Butter
TROLLOPE: Hugh Sykes Davies
WILDE: James Laver
WORDSWORTH: Helen Darbishire

Twentieth Century:
ACHEBE: A. Ravenscroft
ARDEN: Glenda Leeming
AUDEN: Richard Hoggart
BECKETT: J-J. Mayoux
BENNETT: Frank Swinnerton (1950)
BENNETT: Kenneth Young (1975)
BETJEMAN: John Press
BLUNDEN: Alec M. Hardie
BOND: Simon Trussler
BRIDGES: J. Sparrow
BURGESS: Carol M. Dix
CAMPBELL: David Wright
CARY: Walter Allen
CHESTERTON: C. Hollis
CHURCHILL: John Connell
COLLINGWOOD: E. W. F. Tomlin
COMPTON-BURNETT: R. Glynn Grylls
CONRAD: Oliver Warner
DE LA MARE: Kenneth Hopkins
NORMAN DOUGLAS: Ian Greenlees
LAWRENCE DURRELL: G. S. Fraser
T. S. ELIOT: M. C. Bradbrook
T. S. ELIOT: The Making of
    'The Waste Land': M. C. Bradbrook
FORD MADOX FORD: Kenneth Young
FORSTER: Rex Warner

FRY: Derek Stanford
GALSWORTHY: R. H. Mottram
GOLDING: Stephen Medcalf
GRAVES: M. Seymour-Smith
GRAHAM GREENE: Francis Wyndham
HARTLEY: Paul Bloomfield
A. E. HOUSMAN: Ian Scott-Kilvert
TED HUGHES: Keith Sagar
ALDOUS HUXLEY: Jocelyn Brooke
ISHERWOOD: Francis King
HENRY JAMES: Michael Swan
HANSFORD JOHNSON: Isabel Quigly
JOYCE: J. I. M. Stewart
KIPLING: Bonamy Dobrée
LARKIN: Alan Brownjohn
D. H. LAWRENCE: Kenneth Young
(1952)
D. H. LAWRENCE: I:
J. C. F. Littlewood (1976)
LESSING: Michael Thorpe
C. DAY LEWIS: Clifford Dyment
WYNDHAM LEWIS: E. W. F. Tomlin
MACDIARMID: Edwin Morgan
MACKENZIE: Kenneth Young
MACNEICE: John Press
MANSFIELD: Ian Gordon
MASEFIELD: L. A. G. Strong
MAUGHAM: J. Brophy
GEORGE MOORE: A. Norman Jeffares
MURDOCH: A. S. Byatt
NAIPAUL: Michael Thorpe
NARAYAN: William Walsh

NEWBY: G. S. Fraser
O'CASEY: W. A. Armstrong
ORWELL: Tom Hopkinson
OSBORNE: Simon Trussler
OWEN: Dominic Hibberd
PINTER: John Russell Taylor
POETS OF THE 1939-45 WAR:
R. N. Currey
POWELL: Bernard Bergonzi
POWYS BROTHERS: R. C. Churchill
PRIESTLEY: Ivor Brown
PROSE WRITERS OF WORLD WAR I:
M. S. Greicus
HERBERT READ: Francis Berry
SHAFFER: John Russell Taylor
SHAW: A. C. Ward
EDITH SITWELL: John Lehmann
SNOW: William Cooper
SPARK: Patricia Stubbs
STOPPARD: C. W. E. Bigsby
STOREY: John Russell Taylor
SYNGE & LADY GREGORY: E. Coxhead
DYLAN THOMAS: G. S. Fraser
G. M. TREVELYAN: J. H. Plumb
WAR POETS: 1914-18: E. Blunden
EVELYN WAUGH: Christopher Hollis
WELLS: Kenneth Young
WESKER: Glenda Leeming
PATRICK WHITE: R. F. Brissenden
ANGUS WILSON: K. W. Gransden
VIRGINIA WOOLF: B. Blackstone
YEATS: G. S. Fraser

Sir Walter Scott

Scott began his literary career as an editor of the traditional songs and ballads of Scotland and as a writer of romances in verse. In 1814 he published *Waverley*, the first of the series of books which established him as one of the most celebrated writers in Europe. Dr Jack examines Scott's merits as a novelist and his carelessness about the technique of his art; he emphasizes the degree to which Scott's imagination was visual; he traces Scott's part in revolutionizing the status of the novel, and in making mankind more aware than ever before of historical perspectives.

Dr Jack was born in Edinburgh, where his father was a Writer to the Signet and his great-grandfather had been one of Scott's successors as a Clerk of the Court of Session. A Fellow of Pembroke College, Cambridge, and University Lecturer in English, he is the author of *Augustan Satire*, of *English Literature 1815–1832* (the volume of the *Oxford History of English Literature* dealing with the period of Byron, Shelley and Keats), and of *Keats and the Mirror of Art*. He wrote the booklet on Pope which is No. 48 in this Series.

38pp. frontis. bibliog. 140 x 215mm paperback.

The Brontës

In this study in two volumes of the Series subtitled *The Formative Years* and *The Creative Work*, Winifred Gérin shows how in their first period the Brontës produced a collective juvenilia of astounding precocity in which, not only for reasons of age, Charlotte and Branwell were the leading spirits and prolific penmen. This was followed by a lyric period, corresponding to adolescence, of joint poetic output, in which Emily alone excelled, but in which Anne revealed genuine elegiac qualities, and Charlotte emerged as a writer of romantic novelettes already notable for their penetration into motive and character. Finally, after all of them had gained some experience of life, came the great period of novel-writing. . . .

Winifred Gérin is a Fellow and Council Member of the Royal Society of Literature, and has written full-length biographies on each of the four Brontës.

2 vols, plates, bibliog. 140 x 215mm paperback.

WRITERS & THEIR WORK

LONGMAN FOR THE BRITISH COUNCIL

George Eliot

George Eliot (*née* Mary Ann Evans) was thirty-eight when she wrote her first book, *Scenes of Clerical Life*. A few years earlier she had come to London and met the journalist George Lewes who gave her the love and encouragement she needed for the full development of her talent. All her novels were written during her life of 'deep wedded happiness' with Lewes; her last book, *Daniel Deronda*, was published just two years before Lewes's death.

Her genius was immediately recognized by the leading writers of the day, including Dickens and Thackeray. Today she is acknowledged to be one of the great English novelists whose penetrating understanding of character and analysis of motive have had a great influence on the development of the modern novel.

Lettice Cooper is a distinguished novelist and critic with a special interest in the English and European novel of the nineteenth and twentieth centuries, and in the American novel and short story. She is the author of *Robert Louis Stevenson* in the 'English Novelists' Series. Her best-known novels, *The New House*, *National Provincial*, *Three Lives*, and *The Double Heart*, are pictures of English life with its many crosscurrents, religious, political, social, industrial. Her deep interest in these make her particularly able to appreciate the novels of George Eliot.

40pp. frontis. bibliog. 140 x 215mm paperback.

Elizabeth Gaskell

'Her art', says Miriam Allott of Mrs Gaskell, 'is an important, minor achievement.... She still impresses us by the genuineness of her sensibility, the warmth of her personal sympathy, and the liveliness with which she writes about the things which she believed to be important and wanted very much to set right. She is the least stuffy of the Victorians. . . .' This appreciation of the author of *Cranford*, *Wives and Daughters* and *The Life of Charlotte Brontë* will send many to the books themselves: either to refresh their acquaintance or to discover a writer of great perception.

Miriam Allott is Reader in English Literature at Liverpool University. She has also written on Henry James, Emile Brontë and other novelists.

41pp. frontis. bibliog. 140 x 215mm paperback

WRITERS & THEIR WORK

LONGMAN FOR THE BRITISH COUNCIL